Linda L. Simmons, PsyD

Interactive Art Therapy
"No Talent Required" Projects

"*Interactive Art Therapy: 'No Talent Required' Projects* introduces fourteen interactive art directives that the author has used with clients to address a myriad of different issues. Simple in execution yet powerful in symbolic and metaphorical content, these directives help the interacting dyad attend to psychiatric and real-life problems alike through the powerful tool of art. Each chapter introduces a new directive, concluding with a related case vignette to illustrate how one can benefit from the task. This book is a 'how-to' not a 'why.' It is written by a non-art therapist for non-art therapists."

David Gussak, PhD, ATR-BC
Assistant Professor and Clinical Coordinator, Florida State University—Graduate Art Therapy Program

"**B**ehavior change is fraught with encumbrances and complexities, as both clients and therapists know all too well. Bridging the gap between heart and head, external and internal, and insight and action is the essence of the psychotherapeutic process. *Interactive Art Therapy* is a simple, yet powerful tool that heightens clients' underused visual channel for learning and change. The metaphorical and symbolic representation of problems through shared drawings will provide clients with new understanding of the obstacles that keep them stuck, and the various options available to overcome them. This book challenges therapists to work and think more holistically with clients, and to employ their own, underused creativity as treatment technique. Dr. Simmons makes a convincing case that a picture is, in fact, worth a thousand words, and is, perhaps, more powerful in the healing journey!"

David A. Chick, PhD
Psychologist, Hope Psychological Services

More pre-publication
REVIEWS, COMMENTARIES, EVALUATIONS . . .

"Therapists of all types should not be discouraged by the term 'art therapy' in the title of this wonderful book. As the illustrations prove, there is truly no artistic talent required of either the therapist or the client. Instead, simple line drawings are used to present a very basic, commonsense approach to a myriad of common therapeutic issues. The combination of a visual and auditory processing approach to problem solving, as well as the collaborative effort of the therapist with the client, helps the client to gain insight into fears, powerlessness, and ineffective coping strategies. Through a series of activities, the author illustrates techniques for helping clients to overcome stressors, set and achieve goals, and promote personal growth in adverse settings. Each activity is accompanied by a vignette, treatment goals, interventions, and suggestions for follow-up. As I read, I thought of numerous opportunities to use the activities with my current therapy clients and I look forward to sharing the techniques with students."

Kathy DeOrnellas, PhD
Assistant Professor,
Texas Woman's University

The Haworth Press
New York • London • Oxford

NOTES FOR PROFESSIONAL LIBRARIANS AND LIBRARY USERS

This is an original book title published by The Haworth Press, Inc. Unless otherwise noted in specific chapters with attribution, materials in this book have not been previously published elsewhere in any format or language.

CONSERVATION AND PRESERVATION NOTES

All books published by The Haworth Press, Inc., and its imprints are printed on certified pH neutral, acid-free book grade paper. This paper meets the minimum requirements of American National Standard for Information Sciences-Permanence of Paper for Printed Material, ANSI Z39.48-1984.

DIGITAL OBJECT IDENTIFIER (DOI) LINKING

The Haworth Press is participating in reference linking for elements of our original books. (For more information on reference linking initiatives, please consult the CrossRef Web site at www.crossref.org.) When citing an element of this book such as a chapter, include the element's Digital Object Identifier (DOI) as the last item of the reference. A Digital Object Identifier is a persistent, authoritative, and unique identifier that a publisher assigns to each element of a book. Because of its persistence, DOIs will enable The Haworth Press and other publishers to link to the element referenced, and the link will not break over time. This will be a great resource in scholarly research.

Interactive Art Therapy
"No Talent Required" Projects

HAWORTH Practical Practice in Mental Health
Lorna L. Hecker, PhD
Senior Editor

101 Interventions in Family Therapy edited by Thorana S. Nelson and Terry S. Trepper

101 More Interventions in Family Therapy edited by Thorana S. Nelson and Terry S. Trepper

The Practical Practice of Marriage and Family Therapy: Things My Training Supervisor Never Told Me by Mark Odell and Charles E. Campbell

The Therapist's Notebook for Families: Solution-Oriented Exercises for Working with Parents, Children, and Adolescents by Bob Bertolino and Gary Schultheis

Collaborative Practice in Psychology and Therapy edited by David A. Paré and Glenn Larner

The Therapist's Notebook for Children and Adolescents: Homework, Handouts, and Activities for Use in Psychotherapy edited by Catherine Ford Sori and Lorna L. Hecker

The Therapist's Notebook for Lesbian, Gay, and Bisexual Clients: Homework, Handouts, and Activities for Use in Psychotherapy by Joy S. Whitman and Cynthia J. Boyd

A Guide to Self-Help Workbooks for Mental Health Clinicians and Researchers by Luciano L'Abate

Workbooks in Prevention, Psychotherapy, and Rehabilitation: A Resource for Clinicians and Researchers edited by Luciano L'Abate

The Psychotherapist as Parent Coordinator in High-Conflict Divorce: Strategies and Techniques by Susan M. Boyan and Ann Marie Termini

The Couple and Family Therapist's Notebook: Homework, Handouts, and Activities for Use in Marital and Family Therapy by Katherine A. Milewski Hertlein, Dawn Viers, and Associates

The Therapist's Notebook for Integrating Spirituality in Counseling: Homework, Handouts, and Activities for Use in Psychotherapy edited by Karen B. Helmeke and Catherine Ford Sori

The Therapist's Notebook for Integrating Spirituality in Counseling II: More Homework, Handouts, and Activities for Use in Psychotherapy edited by Karen B. Helmeke and Catherine Ford Sori

Interactive Art Therapy: "No Talent Required" Projects by Linda L. Simmons

Therapy's Best: Practical Advice and Gems of Wisdom from Twenty Accomplished Counselors and Therapists by Howard Rosenthal

The Christian Therapist's Notebook: Homework, Handouts, and Activities for Use in Christian Counseling by Philip J. Henry, Lori Marie Figueroa, and David R. Miller

Interactive Art Therapy
"No Talent Required" Projects

Linda L. Simmons, PsyD

The Haworth Press
New York • London • Oxford

For more information on this book or to order, visit
http://www.haworthpress.com/store/product.asp?sku=5397

or call 1-800-HAWORTH (800-429-6784) in the United States and Canada
or (607) 722-5857 outside the United States and Canada

or contact orders@HaworthPress.com

Published by

The Haworth Press, Inc., 10 Alice Street, Binghamton, NY 13904-1580.

PUBLISHER'S NOTE
The development, preparation, and publication of this work has been undertaken with great care. However, the Publisher, employees, editors, and agents of The Haworth Press are not responsible for any errors contained herein or for consequences that may ensue from use of materials or information contained in this work. The Haworth Press is committed to the dissemination of ideas and information according to the highest standards of intellectual freedom and the free exchange of ideas. Statements made and opinions expressed in this publication do not necessarily reflect the views of the Publisher, Directors, management, or staff of The Haworth Press, Inc., or an endorsement by them.

Identities and circumstances of individuals discussed in this book have been changed to protect confidentiality.

Cover design by Kerry E. Mack.

Library of Congress Cataloging-in-Publication Data

Simmons, Linda L.
    Interactive art therapy : no talent required projects / Linda L. Simmons.
        p. cm.
    Includes bibliographical references and index.
    ISBN-13: 978-0-7890-2653-8 (hard : alk. paper)
    ISBN-10: 0-7890-2653-8 (hard : alk. paper)
    ISBN-13: 978-0-7890-2654-5 (soft : alk. paper)
    ISBN-10: 0-7890-2654-6 (soft : alk. paper)
    1. Art therapy. I. Title.

RC489.A7S56 2006
616.89'1656—dc22

                                                                                    2005031512

This book is dedicated to my sons, Samuel and Adam, who have without fail been an encouragement to me over the years, making many personal sacrifices, and always believing that I was capable of completing such a project as this.

ABOUT THE AUTHOR

Linda L. Simmons, PsyD, is currently in private practice at Hope Psychological Services in Lexington, Massachusetts. Dr. Simmons worked for many years in a variety of clinical nursing areas, including psychiatric nursing. From the beginning of her extensive career in psychology, she began combining her hobby of drawing and painting with sound psychological principles in reaching the needs of clients. Dr. Simmons is licensed in Massachusetts and Arkansas and is a member of the American Association of Christian Counselors (AACC) and the Massachusetts Psychological Association.

CONTENTS

Foreword

Rarely do mental health clinicians encounter a book that truly helps clients process information as well as increase insights and change. Seldom do clinicians encounter therapeutic tools that can be used with nearly their entire caseload. Also, one often is not presented a tool to make therapy both fun and useful. Dr. Linda Simmons accomplishes all of these objectives in *Interactive Art Therapy: "No Talent Required" Projects.*

Combining research, theory, and practice, Linda Simmons has compiled a series of activities to use with clients that increases their abilities to communicate and that helps the therapist understand clients at a more profound level than simply through listening. Learning theorists are finding more ways to promote understanding by utilizing as many senses as possible in the learning process. Simmons skillfully employs the interaction between verbal and visual information to increase client learning and change. Her unique therapy techniques facilitate clients' capacities to access available channels for learning and change. Simmons supplies the reader with case vignettes that clearly illustrate the use of her techniques and changes that can occur with their use. She does what most clinicians have difficulty doing: she provides others with insight into specific change techniques in therapy. In addition, because Simmons teaches the reader to increase client learning through dual sensory modes, verbal and visual memory are activated simultaneously, thus enabling the client to be more likely to remember what is learned in therapy.

Inviting even those of us who are the most artistically challenged to make use of drawing with clients, we can look forward to therapy sessions that are both fun and useful for therapist and client alike. The reader will enjoy both the interactive art therapy techniques presented herein, as well as the sensitivity with which Dr. Simmons integrates their use in outcomes as evidenced in the case vignettes. This book is appealing because, indeed, no artistic talent is required to increase one's therapeutic repertoire. The eloquence of Dr. Simmons' work is

Published by The Haworth Press, Inc., 2006. All rights reserved.
doi:10.1300/5397_a

xii INTERACTIVE ART THERAPY

in its simplicity of application. The mental health clinician will both enjoy this book and peruse it often to find ways to increase client learning and change.

Lorna Hecker, PhD
Professor, Marriage and Family Therapy
Director, Couple and Family Therapy Center
Purdue University Calumet
Hammond, Indiana

Preface

This book arose out of the desire to utilize the mental pictures we often get when we're learning or working through new information. As clients talked about their issues in therapy, I found that pictures would often come to my mind. These pictures illustrated the struggle clients were engaged in, the principle of the interventions, and/or the barriers that kept clients from progressing.

Several years ago, I began experimenting with the technique I've come to call Interactive Art Therapy. The sessions in which I used Interactive Art Therapy turned out to be the sessions most remembered by clients. Pictures are something clients can hold onto, either literally with handouts or mentally with images.

We live in an era that encourages professionals to have solid evidence to support any interventions they might use with clients. This is absolutely the right and ethical approach to adopt. Therefore, I also wanted to make sure that whatever techniques I used were well thought out and based on sound clinical principles.

This book explains the concept of Interactive Art Therapy, provides a rationale for the drawings, and demonstrates how to utilize the drawings with clients. It is intended to be a practical book that any therapist can use without needing additional complicated training courses. Many case examples are used throughout the book to illustrate the techniques of Interactive Art Therapy. It should be noted that, although the situations are taken from real life, the individuals in the examples are composites of a number of clients and no one client in particular. Certainly, the stories of particular clients inspired the development of Interactive Art Therapy, but any apparent recognition by clients of their story in this book is coincidental. It indicates identification with commonly seen problems rather than their particular stories as elements of multiple clients' stories were combined into each individual example used in this book.

Published by The Haworth Press, Inc., 2006. All rights reserved.
doi:10.1300/5397_b

Acknowledgments

I would like to acknowledge my husband, Chuck, who has been a support to me in every way, providing time, space, and encouragement for me to write. I would also like to thank my parents, Rollie and Cleta Frazier, for their support and encouragement throughout this project. Janice Pieroni, Esq., has provided editorial support, excellent counsel, and a vision for the future for which I am extremely grateful. Finally, I would like to acknowledge Dr. Lorna Hecker, who was willing to take on a novice writer, believing that the project was worthwhile, guiding things along with kindness and understanding.

Published by The Haworth Press, Inc., 2006. All rights reserved.
doi:10.1300/5397_c

Introduction

As clinicians, we have spent many long hours studying a variety of psychological theories. We have also spent many more hours in supervision learning how to apply these theories to our work with clients. Although clinicians have the educational background to make connections between theory and application, clients seldom do. "Psych lingo" can seem like a foreign language to clients, and, if we're not careful, they can get lost in the mire of their treatment. One way I have found to connect with clients and gain their active participation in the therapeutic process is what I call Interactive Art Therapy. The bridge of using illustrations can be very effective. Most of us are visual learners and seeing our ideas in pictures gives them texture and dimension. Oftentimes, it is the drawings that stick with clients and help them to apply their insights to their everyday lives.

When using drawings to work with clients, it is my goal that the drawings be a tool in an active process. They must be flexible and adaptive to the client's cognitive and developmental abilities. Drawings that are restrictive and inflexible will lead to a therapy session that is frustrating and nonproductive. Clients with average to above-average intelligence will be able to develop and comprehend abstract concepts and symbolism in the drawings. Individuals with below-average intelligence or those with developmental disabilities will need the drawings to be very concrete.

You will likely recall the work of Jean Piaget, a Swiss scientist (b. 1896-d. 1980) whose primary interest was how we acquire intelligence. Through observing his own three children, he began to develop a theory on intellectual development. This theory was laid out in four stages: sensorimotor, preoperations, concrete operations, and formal operations. To gain an understanding of how to tailor Interactive Art Therapy to clients, we must examine Piaget's stages of concrete operations and formal operations.

According to Piaget, children typically enter the concrete operations stage of intellectual development at age seven. Children in this

doi:10.1300/5397_d

stage are capable of placing information into categories and then ordering it, but have difficulty integrating that information into a general explanation. Piaget proposed that children age eleven on through adolescence were able to develop formal operational thinking. In formal operational thinking, children start from a general premise, which includes all possible combinations of information available, and are then able to narrow the focus to specific pieces of information (Kaplan and Sadock, 1989).

Of course, Piaget's theory describes the ideal. The ages at which individuals enter into the stages of intellectual development vary. In fact, some individuals never seem to achieve formal operational thinking abilities even in adulthood. Certainly, individuals with developmental disabilities will not fit nicely into these ideal categories. Therefore, clinicians must be very astute in assessing their clients' intellectual abilities prior to determining how best to present any clinical interventions, including Interactive Art Therapy.

Children and adults who have not entered Piaget's stage of formal operational thinking, for example, will need to work with drawings that have concrete and simple concepts. In addition, they may need more guidance in reaching general conclusions from the specifics of the drawings. Whatever clients' ages, whatever their cognitive and developmental capabilities, clients must be active in the development of the drawings for them to be effective. This is the *art* of using drawings in clinical work.

There are as many drawings as there are ideas, feelings, and imagination. The fascinating and exciting thing about Interactive Art Therapy is that no two drawings are ever exactly alike. Clients' unique stories and solutions will shape and form the drawings. The drawings then develop teaching and learning lessons with lives of their own.

One client, Evelyn, particularly comes to mind. She was a highly intelligent woman and immediately involved herself in Interactive Art Therapy. We had been working on the Coping Arch drawing (see the illustration in Chapter 4). This drawing looks at clients' vulnerabilities, fears, needs for protection, and the pressures imposed by others. Evelyn was thinking in particular of how her family of origin had assaulted her emotionally and how the coping skills she had as a child were inadequate to protect her. The next week, Evelyn came in with a drawing of her own, which was much more elaborate and detailed than what we had done in our therapy session. It was a spider-like drawing in which she was central with no good route for escape. This was a major therapeutic breakthrough for Evelyn as she was able to visualize the position in which her family had placed her. The minimization of her family's destructive behavior toward her stopped. Evelyn kept the drawing, which served as a reminder of her progress.

Evelyn's case also illustrates how Interactive Art Therapy becomes an ongoing creative process. Her drawing's spider-like nature led me to visualize The Spider Web illustration which you will find in Chapter 14. The Spider Web illustration raised questions in my mind such as: "What keeps us 'stuck' in a web of helplessness?"; "Who is the spider that weaves the web?"; and "How can one escape from these feelings of powerlessness?" One thought leads to another and a chain reaction of creativity and insight follow.

The goal of this book is to give a sampling of pictures I have used and to illustrate the therapeutic value of Interactive Art Therapy in working with clients. Drawings can be an excellent bridge between theory and practice.

Few clinicians are artists, nor have many clinicians received specialized training in art therapy. These facts do not need to intimidate therapists or prevent them from exploring the use of this powerful medium in their treatment of clients. It is also important to remember that the task of drawing should not become the focus of the session. Therefore, it is necessary that the pictures used be very simple, basic, and easy to draw. We must always remember that it is the therapeutic process and not the drawings per se that is of benefit to clients.

Practicality is something highly valued by clients. In this age of financial consciousness, clients like to feel they are getting their money's worth. In my experience, the use of Interactive Art Therapy can lead to insight much earlier in treatment than typical "talking" therapies. Seeing with pictures how theory can be practical in their lives makes a great deal of sense to clients. Making sure that practice is based on a rational, well-thought-out plan is highly valued by clinicians. The use of Interactive Art Therapy can be a tool for meeting both those needs.

Chapter 1

Theoretical Foundation for Interactive Art Therapy

For many years, psychotherapy has been thought of as the "talking therapy," primarily using the auditory sensory modality for interacting with clients. Yet, in recent therapeutic history, professionals have been expanding their repertoire, using other sensory modalities to aid clients in the healing process. Dance and movement therapies, music therapy, therapy using photography, various forms of art therapy, and even a therapy using flowers, have all been developed around our primary senses: seeing, hearing, touching, smelling, and tasting. Although many of these therapies seem to work well with clients from an experiential perspective, not all have been thoroughly researched by any means.

It has been reported that more than 50 percent of our cerebral cortex is devoted to visual functions, while a large part of the remaining cerebral cortex capacity is devoted to auditory functions (Basic Behavioral Science Task Force, 1996). Although experientially I knew Interactive Art Therapy worked with clients, as a professional therapist, I wanted to know why. So I began to look at research that might explain this phenomenon. Certainly, the two sensory modalities of seeing and hearing, which are the focus of Interactive Art Therapy, have garnered the highest proportion of research in this area by far.

DUAL-CODING THEORY

Clearly, the underlying notion of Interactive Art Therapy is the interaction between verbal and visual material. When I read the following quote, I had an "aha" moment: "It also should be noted that, under certain circumstances, verbal material can evoke the construction of

Published by The Haworth Press, Inc., 2006. All rights reserved.
doi:10.1300/5397_01

visual representations, and visual material can evoke the construction of verbal representations" (Mayer and Sims, 1994, p. 390). This information comes from a growing body of research investigating the interaction of visual and auditory processes in learning.

The term *multimodal* has been coined to refer to the idea that individuals use more than one sensory modality to learn new material. This concept is part of a larger theoretical framework called dual-coding theory (Mayer and Sims, 1994). Thus far, much of the research done in exploring dual-coding theory has focused on the best way to present academic material to students so they can learn more quickly and retain material longer. In the case of therapy, the new material to be learned and retained is not academic, but new insights into the "why" of behaviors and emotions as well as the development of new coping skills to deal with problematic behaviors and emotions.

The conscious processing of information is necessary to learn new information. It also seems logical to assume that conscious processing is foundational for gaining insight in a therapeutic setting. Conscious processing requires working memory. Recent research suggests that working memory involves the independent functioning of visual processors and auditory processors (Kalyuga et al., 2000; Tindall-Ford et al., 1997). It has also been suggested that the effectiveness of working memory is enhanced with a dual-mode presentation of material rather than a single mode (Moreno and Mayer, 2002; Kalyuga et al., 2000; Tindall-Ford et al., 1997).

Working memory is very important in the therapeutic process. We want clients to remember prior insights, facts, feelings, and thoughts in order to build toward a state of healing and healthier functioning. Interactive Art Therapy takes full advantage of this dual-mode presentation of material in helping clients reach their therapeutic goals.

CONTIGUITY EFFECT

Some have wondered if it matters whether auditory and visual materials are presented separately or together (Tindall-Ford et al., 1997). Mayer and Sims (1994) described a contiguity effect in connection with dual-coding theory. In the simplest terms, they found that auditory and visual material presented simultaneously, the contiguity effect, was the most effective for learning.

This concept was further demonstrated in studies that presented material to students either with words alone or with words and corresponding pictures. The research demonstrated that students remembered significantly more of the information when it was presented in a verbal format along with relevant visual material (Moreno and Mayer, 2002; Kalyuga et al., 2000; Mousavi et al., 1995; Tindall-Ford et al., 1997).

Many therapists use workbook materials and written homework assignments in the therapeutic process. Although these techniques may be effective to a certain extent, the research cited here seems to suggest that the visual material presented in combination with auditory processing might be of greater benefit. In addition, in my experience, it is the exceptional client who will actually follow through and complete written assignments at home without the support and encouragement of having a therapist present.

APPLICATIONS FOR INTERACTIVE ART THERAPY

Interactive Art Therapy certainly reflects a practical application of these research findings in the therapy setting. Being able to process, learn, and remember therapeutic material more effectively means the material is available to build on in session after session. It is also conceivable to suggest that enhancement of the therapeutic process in this way may shorten the course of therapy and lead to longer-lasting positive effects from treatment.

It has been acknowledged for some time that the relationship between therapists and clients in itself is a significant factor in the healing process. Not only does Interactive Art Therapy enhance learning through the dual mode of presenting material, but it also enhances the therapeutic bond between therapists and clients as they collaborate together. This is a special reward for both therapists and clients.

Chapter 2

Cage of Fears

OBJECTIVE

The Cage of Fears illustration is designed to help clients identify the fears that keep them imprisoned. Once identified, this intervention will begin helping them to discover a way out of the cage so that they might experience a new freedom in making life choices.

RATIONALE

Fears are a powerful force that can keep us imprisoned, unable to pursue dreams, goals, relationships, etc. Many of us don't want to admit that we have fears so powerful we can't overcome them without help. Acknowledging fears means exposing personal weaknesses and vulnerabilities. However, exposure is necessary to diagnose the problem accurately and an accurate diagnosis is necessary for effective treatment.

The bars of fear do indeed create a prison and this fact must not be minimized. If minimization occurs, one may escape the cage of iron bars but will do so with chains and shackles that continue to cling. Goals may be reached and tasks accomplished but one will wonder why the load is so heavy and the energy required to move it so great. The joy that should accompany accomplishments melts into sheer exhaustion.

Identifying fears is the first step to diminishing their power. Once the bars of fear are identified, the door can be opened in one of two ways. Doors are kept closed with locks. Typically, the locks are either keyhole locks or combination locks. A key might unlock the door. Keys are equivalent to insight, the "aha" experience, and are more

Published by The Haworth Press, Inc., 2006. All rights reserved.
doi:10.1300/5397_02

likely to work with individuals who have sufficient ego strength to apply their new understanding. They are not so bound by low self-esteem, self-doubt, and feelings of inadequacy.

Combination locks may also be in place to keep the door closed. Usually, three numbers are required to open a combination lock. The search for these three numbers may require much trial and error. It can be tedious work that takes a long time to complete. Individuals who are kept prisoner by combination locks are often so bound by their fears that efforts to free them are achieved in miniscule steps. In other words, long-term psychotherapy may be necessary.

Each client will have different names on the bars of their Cage of Fears. However, the following examples are common.

- Fear of looking foolish
- Fear of failure
- Fear of loneliness
- Fear of not measuring up
- Fear of being criticized
- Fear of being misunderstood
- Fear of death
- Fear of being found out
- Fear of abandonment

Although we most often think of fears in a negative connotation, it is also possible that fears may be necessary for our protection. For example, a fear of water may be healthy if one who doesn't know how to swim is considering jumping into a roaring river. Fear of snakes may be healthy if they are poisonous and one doesn't know how to properly handle them. Similarly, babies placed in playpens with bars may be "imprisoned" for their own safety. Therefore, once fears are identified, we need to determine if they are healthy fears, which serve to protect us from harm, or if they are truly hindering our growth and development.

Once it has been determined that identified fears are a hindrance, clients and therapists can determine a course of action to free the client. Any number of therapeutic techniques may be effective. These include systematic desensitization, assertiveness training, building self-esteem, family therapy, social skills training, etc. It may be helpful for clients who are learning new techniques for managing their fears to go on a "weekend pass" from their Cage of Fears. They will need a chance to try out these new techniques but may not yet have the confidence to follow through consistently. A "weekend pass" gives clients the opportunity to do this and then return to the safety of their cage for evaluation.

It will be important in using the Cage of Fears illustration in therapy that therapists not be perceived as wardens. Wardens are powerful individuals who hold the keys and the combination to the lock. Fears tend to make us vulnerable and dependent. It seems very appealing to have someone stronger take care of us and provide protection. Who wouldn't like such an easy solution to his or her problems? However, as we know, the easy solution is not always the solution that helps us grow and mature. Therapists who take on the role of warden can inadvertently reinforce the fears and dependency. Clients can easily take on the additional fears of, "What if I don't please my therapist?" and/or "What if my feeble attempts at being assertive make me look foolish to my therapist?"

Whatever specific therapeutic techniques are used to deal with fears, clients need to be empowered to open the door themselves. Those who hand them the key or give them the combination numbers to the lock also have the power to lock them up again. This reinforces the underlying premise of Interactive Art Therapy. Clients and therapists must do the work together with therapists taking on the role of coach more often than that of director or teacher (or warden).

CAGE OF FEARS
EXERCISE INSTRUCTIONS

The Cage of Fears is one of the easiest of the Interactive Art Therapy drawings. If you can draw a semistraight line, you've got this one mastered. To begin, therapists draw the cage, as illustrated in Figure 2.1. Once the cage is drawn, therapists then draw a stick figure inside the cage, as in Figure 2.2. A door encloses the stick figure.

Now it is time for clients to work. Clients who are trapped in fear will instantly relate to being locked in a cage. It is explained to clients that each bar of the cage represents one of their fears. Clients are then asked to label each bar of the cage with one of their own fears. Ask clients what it feels like to see themselves caged in by fears with the

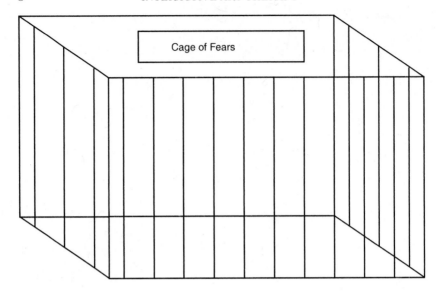

FIGURE 2.1. Sample Cage of Fears.

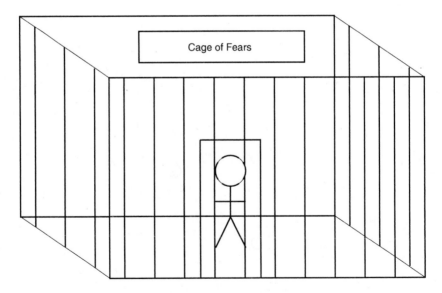

FIGURE 2.2. Cage of Fears with person inside.

door locked tight. This typically evokes strong emotions, which therapists and clients will need to process together.

Next, draw a lock on the door and explain symbolically the way of escape, either with a keyhole or a combination lock. Both therapists and clients will recognize if there is an "aha" experience symbolizing use of the key to unlock the door. For most clients, the combination lock more accurately describes their situation. The combination lock illustration may directly guide the development of clients' treatment plans. Therapists and clients work together to discover the numbers of the combination lock that will unlock the door. The treatment plan will reflect this, with interventions such as journaling, learning social skills, developing assertiveness, systematic desensitization, exploring family-of-origin issues, and others. Some clients will need to confront their fears. Examples might be confronting abusers; establishing boundaries in relationships; or feeling worthy of asking a boss for a raise. As each fear is overcome, clients can imagine that bar of the cage falling over, as in Figure 2.3. Eventually, they will be able to literally see that nothing holds them back from reaching their goals.

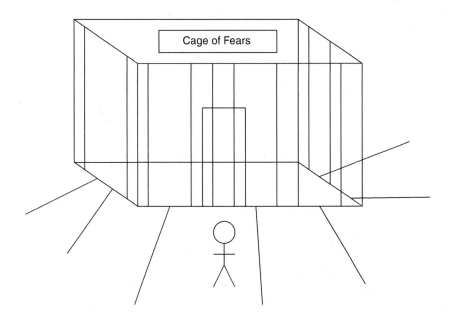

FIGURE 2.3. Individual is released.

VIGNETTE

Martha was a forty-year-old woman who came for therapy because her husband of twenty years was having an affair with a younger woman. Martha had two strong-willed teenage children that she was left to manage alone. Understandably, Martha was devastated and came for therapy because of clinical signs of depression. She was having trouble sleeping, didn't feel like eating, was unable to focus or concentrate, and had thoughts of suicide and feelings of hopelessness. Martha had not worked outside the home since her marriage and was paralyzed with fears about how she would take care of herself and her two children. As if this wasn't enough, Martha's husband was still demanding she cook for his business friends and wasn't quite sure he was ready to move out of their home. He began threatening to stop providing for her financially. Her son, Alan, was staying out late with friends she suspected were using drugs and her daughter, Melinda, was failing two classes. She had previously been an A student.

The first step with Martha was to refer her to her family physician to be evaluated for antidepressant medication. For a couple of weeks, treatment primarily involved crisis management. Once the medication began to help her vegetative signs of depression, Martha was able to begin examining her life. She described her father as a dominating man who didn't easily express any kind of affection. Her mother tolerated this and told Martha that was just the way he was and she shouldn't expect more. So when Martha married, she didn't expect more.

Barry, her husband, seemed so confident and capable at first. He made her feel cared for and protected. But verbal and emotional abuse soon began. "You'll have to stay home with the kids. You're too stupid to get any kind of decent job." After a while, of course, Martha began to believe his messages, which torpedoed her self-esteem.

Barry obviously favored the children over Martha—especially Melinda. By constantly belittling and humiliating Martha in front of the children, he effectively eliminated any respect they ever had for her authority over them as their mother. So when she began having to deal with them alone, they laughed at any attempts she made to enforce rules regarding issues such as curfew and homework. The few times Barry passed through the house during these attempts of Martha to manage the children, he joined them in their laughter. The fears piled up as she realized she had given up all control of her life.

When the Cage of Fears was introduced to Martha in therapy, she began weeping.

MARTHA: That's exactly how I feel! A prisoner in a cage with no way out.

THERAPIST: If you were to name the bars of fear that are keeping you in this cage, what would they be?

MARTHA: There may not be enough bars to name them all. But, for starters, fears of being publicly humiliated, failing, losing my kids, being alone, having to go on welfare because I have no work skills, other people finding out that I'm as stupid as Barry told me I was, losing my home, losing what little self-respect I have left, not being believed that Barry was so mean to me . . .

Martha's tears were flowing freely by this time and it was hard for her to go on.

THERAPIST: Martha, these fears did not begin with Barry. When did they first appear?

MARTHA: You're right. I can't remember when I wasn't afraid of something. Because my dad never showed any affection for my mother and me, I was always afraid he would leave us. I've become like my mom, allowing my husband to walk all over me just to try and keep him at home. I don't know any other way to live.

THERAPIST: There are two ways to escape the Cage of Fears. One way is to unlock the door with a key. That means that just by understanding how the fears developed, you would be able to leave them behind and walk out the door. While I think you're getting the idea of what it means to be imprisoned by your fears, it doesn't seem you'll be able to just get up and walk out the door. That leads up to the other way of escape—the combination lock. There are certain numbers that, in the right combination, will work to unlock the door. We will need to work together to find those numbers.

MARTHA: I see what you mean about the key. It would be great to just be able to use the key and get out as quickly as I can, but my cage is so big and there are so many bars, I can't see myself doing that. How do we find the numbers to the combination lock?

THERAPIST: Martha, I'm so glad you asked. Let's develop a plan together. First of all, are you up for looking more closely at your past to see just how those fears were born?

MARTHA: I'm more than ready. But I know I'll need help. I'm afraid, you know.

Martha and her therapist developed the following treatment plan.

Diagnosis:	Adjustment disorder with anxiety and depressed mood
Goals:	Develop more self-reliance
	Improve self-esteem
	Learn effective parenting skills
	Learn how to manage anxiety and depressive symptoms
Interventions:	Explore past origins of fears
	Assertiveness training
	Parenting skills training
	Social skills training
	Career counseling
	Medication management with primary care physician

Martha and her therapist utilized her treatment plan in examining each bar of fear carefully. After two months in therapy, Martha took the initiative to hire an attorney and examine her options in the marriage. Three months into therapy, she began refusing to entertain her husband's business friends at their home and she began to set limits with the children. The kids were tough and had had their way with Martha for far too long, but after she consistently followed through on consequences for awhile, the situation began to change.

By one year after beginning therapy, Martha was divorced, was working as a cashier in a local department store, and had enrolled in classes at the local community college. Even though she was very bright, Martha voluntarily hired a tutor to help her. It took a long time for Martha to begin throwing off the fears and believe in herself. She consistently went back to the mental image of the Cage of Fears, remembering what it felt like to be imprisoned, and it motivated her to continue onward.

SUGGESTIONS FOR FOLLOW-UP

The Cage of Fears illustration that clients work on may be kept in their files for future use. Nothing is more motivating than going back on occasion to previous work completed and note the progress made. Therapists and clients might also review the illustration regularly and together erase each fear from which clients have been released. How wonderful when the roof of the Cage collapses because it has no bars to support it! Regular review of the Cage of Fears might also reveal a lack of progress and become a vehicle for addressing resistance in therapy. The question might be asked, "Is there some reason clients don't want to escape the Cage even though the fears themselves are unpleasant?"

CONTRAINDICATIONS FOR USE

Because our fears strike so close to the heart of our being, it is very important to determine clients' abilities to manage these strong emotions prior to beginning work with the Cage of Fears. A person must have adequate ego strength to avoid decompensating during this work. Facing some fears will require the development of new coping skills. As an example, individuals fearful of losing their jobs may need concurrent coaching on improvement in their interpersonal skills or help in enrolling in a computer course to update those skills to successfully face this fear head-on.

Therapists must be aware of the deficits that may be keeping the fears going and help clients identify ways to counteract those deficits as much as possible. Otherwise, clients may be overwhelmed with their deep needs. This also highlights the need for clients to have a good support system, hopefully one that includes family, friends, and the community in addition to therapists. Nothing compares to acceptance and caring from others in helping to alleviate the burden of fears.

Chapter 3

Teeter-Totter of Decision Making

OBJECTIVE

One of the most frequent statements therapists hear from clients is, "I just can't make a decision." The implication is usually, "I don't want to be responsible for my decisions" or "I don't want to experience the consequences of my decisions." The Teeter-Totter of Decision Making illustration helps clients clearly see the decision-making process from a variety of angles. This illustration also makes it clear why a balanced approach to decision making leads to greater self-confidence.

RATIONALE

We base our decisions on both internal and external sources of information. External sources include any sources of information that come from without. Examples include spouse, children, friends, coworkers, teachers, pastors, employers, physicians, therapists, dentists, extended family, books, movies, musical lyrics, etc. Internal sources are all the sources of information that come from within. Examples include feelings, thoughts, conscience, dreams, goals, desires, knowledge, past experiences, memories, needs, expectations, perceptions, spirituality, etc. Advantages and disadvantages of utilizing these sources of information exist for both.

The *advantages of external sources* of information are as follows:

- They provide a broader worldview.
- They may have expertise in areas that we lack.
- They may be more objective.

Published by The Haworth Press, Inc., 2006. All rights reserved.
doi:10.1300/5397_03

- They may stimulate our thinking in areas we had ignored or of which we had been unaware.

The *disadvantages of external sources* of information are as follows:

- Each external source has its own agenda.
- Their agendas may or may not be in our best interest.
- External sources may disagree with one another.
- Since each individual is unique, external sources operate on incomplete knowledge of who we are.

The *advantages of internal sources* of information are as follows:

- We are unique creatures. No one else can see things from the exact same perspective as we do.
- We have more control of our internal source of information.
- Internal sources of information are not dependent on on another for harmony.
- Internal sources of information are not lost so easily if we decide not to use them.

The *disadvantages of internal sources* of information are as follows:

- They are limiting and provide a very narrow view of the situation.
- They serve to isolate us from the reactions of others.
- We run the danger of becoming selfish and self-serving.
- The information may be distorted since it isn't tested in the light of social reality.

As you may recall from your kindergarten days, it is not fun to sit on the teeter-totter when it is out of balance. Without being able to adjust the weights of the individuals on the teeter-totter, little to no movement takes place. The fun of playing on a teeter-totter is being able to work together with the other person to achieve maximum movement with ease. When this is accomplished, it seems as if the game can go on endlessly almost without effort. When we can learn this type of flexibility to adjust to varying situations, decision making can take on this same free-floating quality.

TEETER-TOTTER OF DECISION MAKING
EXERCISE INSTRUCTIONS

First of all, therapists draw a balanced teeter-totter as shown in Figure 3.1. Clients are then asked to identify their external sources of information that might be utilized in decision making and list them on one side of the teeter-totter, as shown in Figure 3.2. In the same manner, clients identify their internal sources of information, as in Figure 3.3.

Together, therapists and clients examine these sources of information and decide which side of the teeter-totter has the most weight. Frequently, clients are shocked at how much they depend on one side or the other. When we depend on either end of the spectrum more than the other, the results can be damaging.

Individuals who rely excessively on external sources of information find they frequently experience feelings of insecurity, fear, anxiety, confusion, powerlessness, low self-esteem, and self-doubt (see Figure 3.4). Since they can't read the minds of their external sources, they're never quite sure what they'll hear. In order to continue receiving information from external sources, one must please them most of the time. If the external sources don't agree with one another, the dilemma of who's most important to keep happy arises. An emotional roller-coaster ride is often the result.

On the other hand, if individuals rely too heavily on internal sources of information, they might experience loneliness, insecurity, narcissistic thoughts, a lack of trust, and isolation (see Figure 3.5).

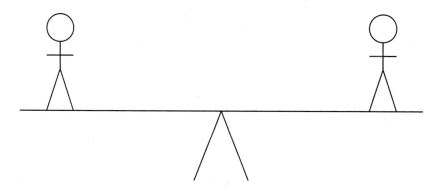

FIGURE 3.1. Balanced teeter-totter.

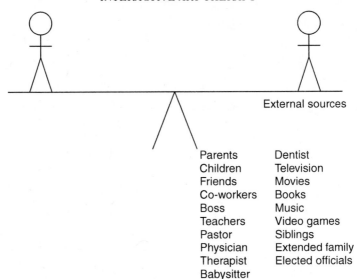

Parents	Dentist
Children	Television
Friends	Movies
Co-workers	Books
Boss	Music
Teachers	Video games
Pastor	Siblings
Physician	Extended family
Therapist	Elected officials
Babysitter	

FIGURE 3.2. Identifying external sources of information.

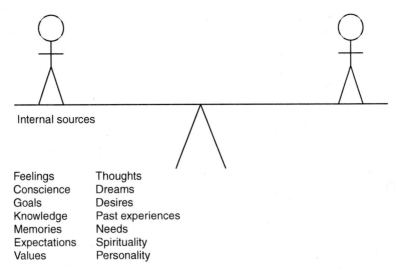

Feelings	Thoughts
Conscience	Dreams
Goals	Desires
Knowledge	Past experiences
Memories	Needs
Expectations	Spirituality
Values	Personality

FIGURE 3.3. Identifying internal sources of information.

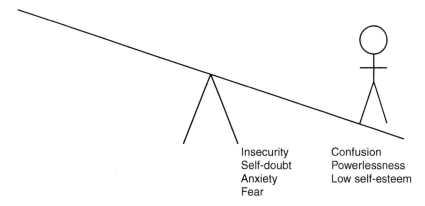

Insecurity   Confusion
Self-doubt   Powerlessness
Anxiety   Low self-esteem
Fear

FIGURE 3.4. Emphasis on external sources.

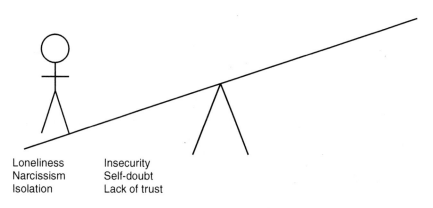

Loneliness   Insecurity
Narcissism   Self-doubt
Isolation   Lack of trust

FIGURE 3.5. Emphasis on internal sources.

These individuals have nothing with which to compare their internal sources and thus they can't judge how others will receive their decisions. External sources of information might feel rejected when they see that their opinions aren't appreciated or valued. Thus, people who think all the information they need to make decisions is within themselves may find themselves very lonely indeed. They can also become very rigid and narrow in their worldview.

How to shift the weight on the teeter-totter guides therapists and clients in developing a treatment plan. The shifts often have to be completed in small segments, depending on how much clients have relied on one type of information. If clients are excessively dependent, any shift in the other direction may feel to them like they're going to fall off the teeter-totter. They could react by clinging to the familiar end of the teeter-totter more than ever.

VIGNETTE

Mary was a twenty-eight-year-old woman who was newly married to Robert. Their courtship had been smooth sailing. However, after six months of marriage, Robert and Mary found that they were becoming more and more tense with each other. Frequently, they got into arguments that sent Mary off crying to her room. When the therapist asked Mary about the source of their arguments, Mary replied that Robert wanted her to take on more of the family finance management. Mary had assumed Robert would handle this task and make the necessary decisions.

The therapist asked Mary who made the decisions during their courtship. She described a scenario where she almost always deferred to Robert and he seemed pleased to be in the protector role. This changed when they immediately bought a new home and Robert was feeling pressured with all the responsibilities of marriage. Mary felt that his requests for her to share in family responsibilities were reasonable, but she became paralyzed when it came to making any decisions on her own.

THERAPIST: Mary, who made the decisions in your family of origin?

MARY: Mostly my father.

THERAPIST: Didn't your mother ever make decisions for herself—even small ones?

MARY: She didn't dare. He even told her what groceries to buy. If she made any meals he didn't like, he would dump the food down the garbage disposal, storm out of the house, and go to the local café for dinner. A couple of times she tried to speak up and got a plate of food in her face.

THERAPIST: Your father doesn't sound like a very nice man.

MARY: An understatement. I learned very early in my life to do as I was told.

THERAPIST: How did you learn this lesson?

MARY: I'm not sure I'm ready to talk about that. Let's just say I got hurt when I didn't obey.

It came out later in therapy that Mary had been sexually abused by her father from the ages of four to twelve. She later admitted that if she didn't submit willingly to her father's demands, she would be beaten.

THERAPIST: Mary, it sounds like you learned that making decisions could be a very dangerous proposition. Let's see if we can illustrate this dilemma with a drawing.

Mary identified the internal and external sources of information that she would have available for making decisions, shown in Figure 3.6.

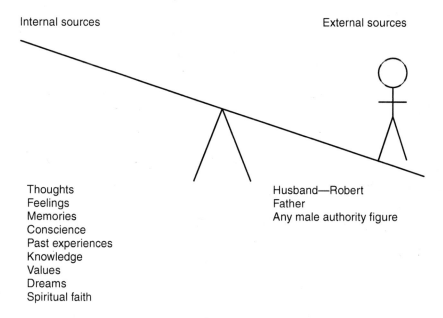

Internal sources

External sources

Thoughts
Feelings
Memories
Conscience
Past experiences
Knowledge
Values
Dreams
Spiritual faith

Husband—Robert
Father
Any male authority figure

FIGURE 3.6. Mary's internal and external sources for making decisions.

Although Mary obviously had many internal resources upon which she could draw, she and her therapist discovered that she consistently depended on external sources to guide her. Initially, Mary was quite surprised at what she saw, but in light of her family history, it all made sense. With the Teeter-Totter of Decision Making illustration to guide them, the therapist and Mary together developed the following treatment plan.

Diagnosis:	Post-traumatic stress disorder
	Dependent personality disorder
Goals:	Resolve past abuse issues from family of origin
	Develop communication skills that she could use with her husband
	Improve ability to make decisions with confidence
	Improve self-esteem
Interventions:	Explore past abuse that contributed to her current marital problems
	Learn and practice communication skills
	Assertiveness training
	Marital therapy after progress was made on individual goals
	Practice making decisions using the Teeter-Totter of Decision Making illustration

As Mary and her therapist examined her history of sexual abuse, it quickly became clear to Mary why she had so much trouble making decisions. She also readily saw that she was expecting reactions from Robert similar to those that she got from her father, even though Robert had no pattern of reacting in that way. The other insight that jumped out at Mary from looking at the illustration was how little she valued her own internal sources of information. With some assertiveness training and communication skills under her belt, her marriage improved almost immediately. Robert was amenable to working on the marital issues with her and both were happy with the results. Of course, the exploration and resolution of past abuse issues took longer, but Mary was encouraged to persevere until she made significant progress in that area as well.

SUGGESTIONS FOR FOLLOW-UP

Understandably, Mary initially felt uncomfortable scooting farther down the teeter-totter to gain a more balanced perspective in making decisions. She needed lots of encouragement and support, as she often felt like she was falling off. The Teeter-Totter of Decision Making illustration was kept handy in her file and with each successful attempt to be more assertive, it was noted on her drawing. Eventually, a series of drawings were developed and Mary was astonished after a year to look back at how the drawings had evolved into a balanced teeter-totter. The fulcrum maintaining the balance was made of self-confidence in her newly developed skills.

Once clients have worked through the decision-making process with this technique, allow them an opportunity to "try it out." After implementation of their decisions, process in therapy what were the consequences of their decisions. Questions to be explored might be, "What did it feel like to be decisive?" "Were you satisfied with the outcome?" "How did others perceive you in this new role?" and "How did you perceive yourself in a decisive role?"

CONTRAINDICATIONS FOR USE

Just as an actual teeter-totter feels insecure and frightening when out of balance, clients will feel the same way when their lives are out of balance. The fear of falling to the ground and sustaining injury when trying to make adjustments is genuine. Therapists need to realize this and provide supports with each adjustment. Without the proper emotional and psychological supports in place, clients may "freeze" and be unable to continue with their progress. Thus, therapists must pace the sessions carefully when using the Teeter-Totter of Decision Making illustration so that clients feel challenged but not overwhelmed.

It is important not to send clients forth armed with a new technique unless they have been supplied with all the tools they need to be successful. Besides an understanding of the decision-making process, clients will likely need assertiveness training to follow through on decisions they've made. Clients who have been dependent on others to make decisions for them will need to be able to break those dependency ties in a healthy manner and continue. Clients who have primarily made decisions based on their own internal feedback may need help developing socialization skills in order to approach others for input.

Chapter 4

The Coping Arch

OBJECTIVE

The Coping Arch is an illustration that allows individuals to visualize how they develop particular styles of coping mechanisms in relationships. Once those coping mechanisms are identified, this illustration can be used to discuss their current effectiveness. The effective coping mechanisms can be reinforced and new ones learned where needed.

RATIONALE

As human beings, we were created to be social. Few individuals are happy and content being hermits. We typically seek out others similar to ourselves with whom we would like to interact. Most of us have a deep inner longing to be known by others and be unconditionally accepted regardless of our flaws. In an ideal world, we can completely accept others in return, arms outstretched with no fear of harm. The closest we may come to seeing this type of human interaction take place is with toddlers. Of course, infancy and the toddler years are jam packed with growth, with the accomplishment of new skills occurring almost on a minute-by-minute basis. In a secure, loving home, toddlers can display their new achievements without fear to an adoring audience. Their family members will clap, cheer, and encourage them even when the diaper hits the ground.

This type of environment provides the acceptance a toddler needs to let everything about him or her be known. As soon as they can talk, we begin hearing, "Look at me; see what I can do!" "Watch me!" or "I bet you can't do this!" Toddlers are proud of themselves and want

Published by The Haworth Press, Inc., 2006. All rights reserved.
doi:10.1300/5397_04

their world to know it! In a loving home, it hasn't occurred to them that they should be afraid to display their many talents or that others might make fun of their less-than-perfect attempts at something new. However, even in the best of homes, parents get tired from too much laundry, too many dirty dishes, and too many long hours at work. Every now and then, even the best of parents give a cranky reply and aren't really interested in anything except a warm shower. The toddler will begin to assess situations a little more carefully before giving a totally spontaneous performance.

Once children begin to have more interactions with individuals outside their own home (such as in preschool or at a babysitter's), they begin to realize that they may not be the center of the universe. As kind and attentive as most adults are to toddlers, in more public settings, they likely have several toddlers who want to be the center of attention. Enthusiasm may not be so readily available. As children enter school, they will likely begin to experience that some kids can be cruel by teasing and even bullying, for example. Not all adults will be as forbearing as their parents. They begin to develop fears around what might happen if they are fully and completely known by others. Those fears form the first arch, which in adulthood becomes a barrier to being fully available to others. Examples of common fears that people experience when they contemplate being fully known by others include the following:

- Being smothered
- Abandonment
- Failure
- Rejection
- Being ridiculed
- Being misunderstood
- Not measuring up
- Being disappointed
- Being humiliated
- Being criticized
- Found to be unlovable

These fears are also unacceptable to display to others. For others to be aware of our fears makes us vulnerable. Survival requires that our vulnerabilities be concealed and protected as much as possible.

We then form a second arch, which consists of all the coping mechanisms we use to protect our vulnerabilities and our inner self. These coping mechanisms allow us to show the world only what we want it to see or only what we consider safe. Coping mechanisms, of course, are tailored to our own peculiar self-characteristics and our unique vulnerabilities. Over time, we try out different ways of coping and keep that arsenal of coping mechanisms that have been reinforced as being effective. These arches become an umbrella that we hope will keep out potential assaults that could result from being fully known. Examples of common coping mechanisms include the following:

- Withdrawal
- Isolating
- Intellectualizing
- Being "good"
- Avoiding risks
- Becoming over-responsible
- Suppression of feelings
- Alcoholism and drug addiction
- Procrastinating
- Sarcasm
- Having a "tough" exterior
- Sleep
- Over-/undereating
- Becoming a "people pleaser"
- Exercise
- Doing the "bare minimum" to get by

In spite of our best efforts, people will still want to get to know us for various reasons. Some people are genuinely kind, generous people who want the enjoyment of relationship. Others have darker motives and may be abusive, vindictive, and angry. Many have mixed motives.

Typically, in spite of the need for self-protection, the innate need we have to relate to others and be known as we were in our toddler years will motivate us to let down some of the barriers. This becomes a problem if we are lacking in discernment and let in *anyone* who knocks at our personal door. "Anyone" includes angry, critical, and abusive people as well as those who are encouraging, supportive, and loving. Inevitably, we will experience pain from negative relationships. A common reaction is to rebuild the arches thicker than ever. However, this keeps out people who might provide us with rich, satisfying relationships. Loneliness results.

The solution is learning about trust—who is trustworthy and to what extent that trustworthiness goes. After a discussion on how one learns to trust, the Coping Arch illustration becomes an excellent tool to discover how we use our coping mechanisms to either let people through our barriers or keep them out. In reality, only a few coping mechanisms are completely unhealthy in all situations. Examples of those would include alcoholism, drug addictions, self-harm behaviors, and violence toward others. Most coping mechanisms have a useful purpose when used at the right time, at the right place, in the right situation, and with the right person.

When a person is totally focused on self-protection, they frequently use the coping mechanisms in their arsenal indiscriminately. Although this may serve a self-protective function, it doesn't serve the function of screening people for possible satisfying relationships. For instance, withdrawal is a common coping mechanism that people use for self-protection. It is extremely difficult to get an individual to give up a coping mechanism that has worked in some way for years. Rather than telling an individual to get rid of this method of self-protection, teach him or her to use it in a discerning manner. To withdraw from a relationship may be quite healthy if the other individual is angry or abusive. Withdrawal for these types of people may be for a short time until they make some positive changes, or it may need to be permanent. However, using withdrawal to protect oneself from a friendly, encouraging person is self-defeating. Even in this situation, the friendly person might tend to be overbearing. The use of mild withdrawal might serve to keep this positive relationship in a healthy balance.

The Coping Arch illustration is a very visual way in which to help individuals begin to see the nuances of relationships. This is certainly an art that is difficult to learn. For clients who have been in abusive or unsatisfying relationships in the past, it is difficult for them to imagine the ebb and flow involved in relating to others and how to use their coping mechanisms to monitor that movement.

THE COPING ARCH
EXERCISE INSTRUCTIONS

Begin this illustration by drawing your best stick figure in the lower left-hand corner of the page as in Figure 4.1.

Ask the client to describe himself or herself in as much detail as he or she is willing to divulge. Instruct the client that you are looking for descriptive words related to all aspects of who he or she is, both positive and negative (see Figure 4.2). At some point, they may need the help of the therapist, who can certainly describe characteristics of the client he or she has observed in the therapy sessions. Often, clients with low self-esteem, for example, will get stuck on only the negative qualities they see in themselves. A narcissist, on the other hand, will avoid any qualities with a negative connotation. Don't push clients too hard on this. If it's early in the therapeutic relationship, they may

FIGURE 4.1. Stick figure for Coping Arch exercise.

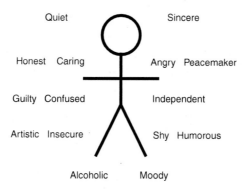

FIGURE 4.2. Examples of descriptive words, positive and negative.

still be wary of how much of themselves they want to reveal to the therapist.

Present to the client the explanation given earlier in this chapter on our innate desire to be fully known by others in relationships. Describe how toddlers like to display their new abilities and how fears develop as we discover that others may not see us as the center of the universe. Then draw the first arch, labeling it as the fears we develop to protect our inner selves. Have the client label the fears he or she experiences when he or she contemplates what it would be like to be fully known by others (as in Figure 4.3).

Next, explain how we typically don't want others to find out about our fears, which make us vulnerable. Draw the second arch and help the client identify the various coping mechanisms he or she uses to protect himself or herself from discovery of fears and of being fully known (see Figure 4.4).

After this task is completed, draw multiple stick figures to the right of the coping arches. Draw an arrow from each stick figure toward the arches as if they were trying to penetrate the defenses (see Figure 4.5). Along the shaft of each arrow, write a general overall quality of someone who might want to gain access to us. Mix the qualities up to represent both positive and negative characteristics. Discuss with the client various ways these people might try to gain access to the client's inner self and also the possible motivations for wanting to do so.

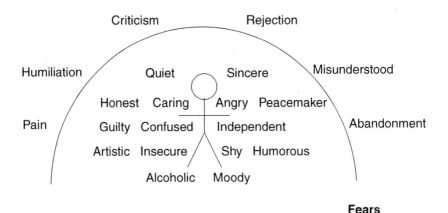

FIGURE 4.3. Above the arch are shown the fears some have of being fully known by others.

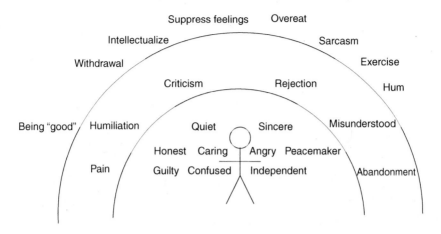

FIGURE 4.4. Coping mechanisms are shown in the outer arch.

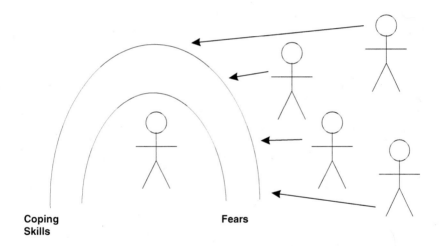

FIGURE 4.5. People who might want to gain access to the individual under the arch.

Many times, people who have operated from a primarily defensive stance by using their coping mechanisms to protect themselves from their fears and from being known, need to develop awareness of others and begin to see relationships from different perspectives. This step begins that process in a visual way.

Next, ask the client if he or she can describe examples of what has happened in his or her life when loneliness has taken over and he or she has invited others in too quickly. Typically, hurt feelings, disappointments, and disillusionment arise out of this discussion. Most of the time, clients will admit that their reactionary behavior is to kick everyone out and vow never to allow that kind of pain to happen again. (However, the pain of loneliness and isolation becomes just as bad, if not worse.) Allow the client to process those feelings as long as necessary. This often really gets at the heart of why clients with this type of problem are in the therapist's office. The insight and understanding gained from this step will be the turning point for making positive change.

Present to the client that positive changes will occur and satisfying relationships will result when he or she learns to distinguish who is trustworthy and the extent to which that trust can be taken. Spending some time on the topic of trust is important at this time. Many people have the perspective that a person is either trustworthy or not and that no middle ground exists. It is important for the client to begin to understand that trust operates on a continuum and is not an all-or-nothing proposition.

Finally, the Coping Arch illustration can be used to help the client take an offensive and confident approach to building satisfying relationships by analyzing his or her coping mechanisms in an assertive manner. When used in a defensive manner, coping mechanisms tend to take over our lives at will. Using coping mechanisms in an assertive manner means the client decides if that mechanism is effective in the current situation with the particular person he or she is dealing with. Each of the identified coping mechanisms should be analyzed to determine if there might be any positive uses. Once this is done, the therapist and client together may decide that some coping mechanisms need to be eliminated altogether, such as excessive alcohol use. They might also decide that some new coping mechanisms might be beneficial and worthwhile to learn. The Coping Arch illustration can be modified over time to reflect the deletions and additions of coping mechanisms.

VIGNETTE

Tom made the decision to attend therapy sessions because he had just been overlooked for a job promotion a second time. He was a computer engineer and had a very impressive résumé. No one doubted that Tom knew his stuff when it came to developing a new software product. Everyone wanted Tom on their production team, but no one wanted him to be their boss. In addition, no one wanted to socialize with Tom after work—any camaraderie stopped when the work day ended. He felt distant from his wife of ten years and was uncertain as to how much longer his marriage might last.

It wasn't that relationships weren't important to Tom; he just didn't know how to establish them or maintain them. Tom realized that the few "friends" he had made over the years tended to use his intellect and abilities for their own betterment but left him feeling emotionally empty. He even recognized that his wife found his income more attractive than his personality. Bottom line: Tom was lonely but he didn't know how to engage with people in a mutually satisfying way.

THERAPIST: Tom, I understand you're coming to therapy because of unsatisfactory relationships in many areas of your life.

TOM: Bluntly put, that's right. But the thing is, I want relationships and I try very hard to be friendly. I'm clueless about how I can be so smart in my work and such a failure relationally.

THERAPIST: It's not an uncommon problem. Your work requires a lot of analytical thinking, which is obviously one of your strengths. Let's use that asset and see if we can analyze together through a drawing what might be at the bottom of this.

TOM: That sounds interesting. Let's do it.

THERAPIST: First of all, I'd like you to describe yourself—both positive and negative qualities.

TOM: Well, people call me a nerd and an egghead. My wife says I'm a space cadet . . .

THERAPIST: Let's begin again. I want to hear how *you* would describe *yourself.*

TOM: Okay. . . . Well, I'm nice and try to be friendly. I enjoy mental challenges. I'm a husband and a computer engineer. I like riding my bike.

THERAPIST: Tom, I know this is just our second session and I don't want you to reveal more about yourself than you feel comfortable doing, but I'm wondering if you could describe more of who you are in addition to what you do.

TOM: I'll try, but that's tough. Now that I think about it, maybe that question reveals some of what you're asking. I feel uncomfortable talking about myself much. I guess I'm insecure and lack confidence in myself a lot of the time. I get angry easily and could really blow up at people if I let myself. Now, this is a little embarrassing, but I get very emotional when I listen to classical music. I always wanted to learn how to do ballroom dancing but I'm very clumsy.

See Figure 4.6 for the beginning of Tom's arch illustration.

THERAPIST: Well, that's a great start. We can always add to that list over time. Now, I want you to think about your two-year-old niece. Remember how eager she is for everyone to notice all her new accomplishments? But even though she can jump, a two-year-old doesn't have it mastered. Yet she longs to hear your acceptance and approval anyway. Human beings at any age long for that unconditional acceptance and approval by other human beings. Let's face it: we are social creatures and we want to feel that we "fit in" no matter what. Although your niece's family likely gives her that approval on a fairly consistent basis, even the best of parents get grumpy after problems at the office and don't want to hear another "Look at me!" It is the beginning of recognition that there are times when the approval I'm seeking won't be there.

TOM: I know exactly what you mean! My sister had the flu last week and wasn't feeling well. My niece, Grace, wanted her mom to

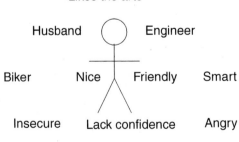

FIGURE 4.6. Tom's self-description.

watch her throw a ball and my sister responded by saying not now and rolled back over in bed. Grace's face fell and she looked like she'd lost her best friend.

THERAPIST: That's right. And the older we get, the more we learn that our feelings will get hurt and we're not the center of the universe to most other people. We begin to develop fears about what might happen if we reveal to others what's in our innermost being. Tom, what are you afraid will happen if someone tries to get to know you intimately?

TOM: I'm afraid of being rejected and I'm afraid of the humiliation if I should be rejected in public. I would rather have no friends at all than for that to happen. It's hard to say, but it's the truth.

See Figure 4.7 for Tom's associated fears.

THERAPIST: I know it's hard to say. And that's why we try to keep our fears hidden. They make us feel very vulnerable. We develop ways to cope that protect both our innermost self and the fears that keep us vulnerable. These coping mechanisms cover us like the arch of an umbrella. What are the ways you cope, Tom?

TOM: Mainly, I keep my distance from people. I work long hours and stay to myself. I try to avoid sharing feelings with others at all costs. Now that I think about it, even my hobbies are things I can do alone—reading and gardening.

See Figure 4.8 for Tom's coping mechanisms.

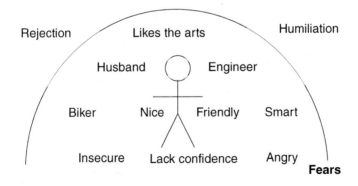

FIGURE 4.7. Tom's fears.

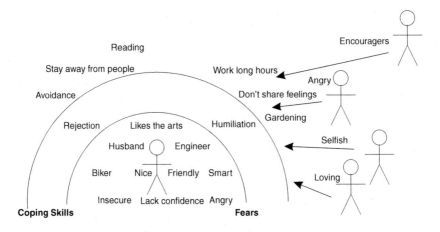

FIGURE 4.8. Coping skills are shown in the outer layer.

THERAPIST: Those are great connections you've made, Tom. I've noticed that even here in the office, it's hard for you to maintain eye contact, and when you began to share about these sensitive issues, you turned away from me in your chair. If I were someone considering a friendship, I might easily get the idea you weren't interested. But regardless of the ways you self-protect, others want to get to know your inner self, and for a variety of reasons. Of course, people are complex, but some may be primarily selfish, some angry, some encouraging, some loving, and so forth (see Figure 4.8). They each have their own motives and agenda for wanting to get to know you. You have already admitted that you get lonely. Can you ever remember a time when you let your guard down and all different types of people got through your defenses?

TOM: Can I ever! It was unforgettable and I haven't opened up since. I was so lonely in college after leaving home for the first time that I decided to accept an invitation to a fraternity party. After a couple of drinks, I began to tell all the guys there about the disasters of my first date. They all began laughing and I realized they were laughing *at* me and not *with* me. I overheard one guy say, "Can't you just see the geek with braces trying to kiss this girl? We should set him up with Julie and see if he's still got it!" I ran out of the party and I've never opened up about anything since.

THERAPIST: And never opening up has brought you to this current place of unbearable loneliness. I can't fully imagine the pain you must have experienced at that party, but I know your reaction has kept many people out of your life, people with whom you might have developed very satisfying relationships.

The therapist worked with Tom at this point on how to understand trust in the development of relationships. Tom eventually recognized that he had allowed that one experience to form his opinion that trust is an all-or-nothing entity. He was an eager student in learning that trust comes in degrees and changes with different people, in different situations, and at different times. He began to see the implications of how his need to self-protect and his inability to trust appropriately had been affecting every relational situation in his life.

THERAPIST: Tom, many of the coping mechanisms you've developed over the years are good ones and have done their job to protect you. However, I think you can now be more discriminative in how you use them. For example, withdrawal is quite effective in protecting you from critical people, but maybe you only need it for a period of time until you formulate a plan for productive confrontation. If you were to go to a party now, you might withdraw for a time until you could observe how people interact with each other. You might then determine that there are those individuals with whom you would enjoy developing a friendship and drop the withdrawal tactic and others whom you can see have different values and you would choose to maintain the withdrawal stance.

TOM: I get it! I've been allowing the withdrawal tactic to take over my life. You're suggesting that I take control and use it as a tool rather than just hide under it as if it were a blanket. I can't wait to look at the other coping mechanisms and analyze them. I've never felt like I had so much power in relationships before!

THERAPIST: It does bring about an exciting shift when we recognize the coping mechanisms can be tools we use for our benefit rather than weapons that often backfire against us. We may find some gaps and instances in which we need to help you develop all new coping mechanisms and other instances in which some of the coping mechanisms in your arsenal are serving no productive purpose and need to be dropped altogether.

It actually took several weeks for Tom to work through the Coping Arch illustration. However, at the end of the process, Tom saw clearly why and how he had been keeping people at a distance. He gained insight into how his need for excessive self-protection negatively affected his work relationships and his marriage. The Coping Arch illustration then became a vehicle for strategizing about positive changes he could make in his life.

Diagnosis:	Adjustment disorder, unspecified
	Avoidant personality disorder
Goals:	Development of effective social skills
	Resolve past emotional damage, which led to social withdrawal
	Development of assertive communication skills
	Improvement in self-esteem
Interventions:	Exploration of past emotional damage
	Assertiveness training
	Learn effective social skills appropriate for both the work setting and family life
	Marital therapy after progress on individual goals
	Development and practice of friendship skills
	Help Tom find ways and places to expand his social network outside of work and home

Tom began to see a whole new world of possibilities in social settings. Tom worked on the skill development side of therapy with gusto, practicing during sessions and gradually building his confidence to the point that he began to take social risks independently. His self-esteem became more positive and he felt more powerful in making relationship choices. With his new insights and understandings behind him, he became more open to relationships in a variety of settings. He became hopeful that his job and marriage might take on greater depth, leading to more personal satisfaction.

SUGGESTIONS FOR FOLLOW-UP

Tom had built up such an avoidant style in dealing with social situations over the years that initially he was quite reluctant to take any social risks. This avoidant style had been reinforced through many personal rejections and failures. As Tom became better prepared to try out his new social skills in the real world, his therapist had to help him find low-risk situations initially, ones in which the lack of success wouldn't be overly crushing. The therapist found it helpful to teach Tom how to evaluate these social situations for himself, both the likelihood of success and how to accurately assess the outcome of failures. Tom also learned how to look for evidence indicating the trustworthiness of individuals with whom he might want to socialize.

Periodic reevaluation using the Coping Arch illustration is encouraging and instructive for clients. As they modify and/or add new coping skills to the outer arch, eliminate fears from the inner arch, and modify and/or add new aspects to their own personal makeup, people begin to see themselves become stronger in relating to others. As they begin to more accurately evaluate the trustworthiness and possible motives of others, they gain confidence in their ability to handle social situations.

CONTRAINDICATIONS FOR USE

This illustration has more steps and is more complex than some of the others and may be more difficult to use with those who are cognitively challenged. The therapist might accommodate for this by going slower and making sure that each step is clearly understood before proceeding to the next step. Also, keeping the personal characteristics, fears, and coping mechanisms to a basic minimum in this situation would be helpful.

Some people who are seeking help with relationship issues might be too close to an extremely painful situation. For example, someone who has experienced a broken engagement the week prior to their first therapy session might be grieving too deeply to be able to engage in the more global perspective this illustration requires. Individuals experiencing a major depression might have difficulty with the more complex analysis of this illustration. In situations like these, crisis treatment and stabilization will be necessary before this illustration can be successfully used to help the client develop healthier relationships.

Chapter 5

Boundary Castle

OBJECTIVE

No feeling is worse than that of powerlessness in relationships. Self-esteem plummets when we feel that we are "fair game" for anyone who might want to take advantage of our weaknesses. The Boundary Castle illustration clearly demonstrates what happens when we allow others unlimited access to our lives and demonstrates how to take the steps necessary to regain control.

RATIONALE

Most individuals have an awareness of the amount of personal space they need between themselves and others in order to feel comfortable and safe. For close, trusted family members, that distance might be quite minimal. For strangers, the need for personal space might be extensive. Of course, various gradations are in between, depending on our level of trust and experience with the people involved. Individuals with a healthy sense of self-identity and positive self-esteem will be able to successfully negotiate this concept of personal space most of the time. On the occasions in which they get "fooled" regarding someone's trustworthiness, they are able to evaluate the situation and make the necessary adjustments in order to feel comfortable and safe once again.

Two categories of other individuals have great difficulty understanding the concept of personal space and/or implementing or setting appropriate limits. The first category includes those rare individuals who are naive and inexperienced in life. They seem to embrace the core belief that everyone is honest and trustworthy. These individ-

Published by The Haworth Press, Inc., 2006. All rights reserved.
doi:10.1300/5397_05

uals are crushed when they act on that core belief, allowing everyone into their most intimate personal space, and discover that their core belief isn't true. The second category of people who have problems with personal space are those who have been victimized in one way or another. Abuse and mistreatment have taught them that they have no rights or abilities to set limits on who enters their personal space. When these individuals try to set limits, they tend to be ineffective, inconsistent, and expectant of failure.

In the Boundary Castle illustration, the castle walls represent the limits we set on our personal space. The moat surrounding the castle represents the defense mechanisms we might typically use to protect ourselves from attack by those who don't have our best interests at heart. It might seem difficult for some to understand how a seemingly impregnable fortress such as a castle could fail to provide protection. However, the characteristics of the defender are the real determinants for the strength of the castle. Self-doubt, fear, denial, and a desire to avoid pain are only some of the obstacles the defender must contend with in order to defend his or her castle.

The inhabitant of the castle might be a "damsel in distress" or a "knight in shining armor." Gender is not binding in either of these roles. Damsels in distress are individuals who feel so helpless they don't utilize the defenses they have available. They frequently let the drawbridge down at inopportune times, hoping that those approaching the castle won't be enemies. They fail to take the necessary precautions needed to protect themselves and may feel they get what they deserve when the outcome goes against them. Damsels in distress feel powerless to take care of themselves and are constantly hoping that someone will rescue them.

The knight in shining armor clearly knows where the perimeter of safety is located and is prepared to defend that perimeter if needed. Many qualities combine to make knights successful in their quest to defend themselves against any enemies who might challenge their safety. For one thing, knights wear protective clothing. They know they must trust their intelligence and remain alert at all times. They prepare and practice in advance of the need for protection. They are aware of their surroundings and are therefore aware of any threat that might approach. If necessary, they fortify their castle walls. They do not hesitate to enlist the aid of other knights if they fear being overwhelmed by the attacking force. Knights make sure they have adequate supplies on hand for good self-care. Finally, knights know how to assess a situation to determine if all this is necessary or if it's safe to have some "R & R" time.

The Boundary Castle illustration makes good use of this vivid imagery in helping clients understand the concept of boundaries or healthy limits to personal space. It will also help them recognize the need to employ wisdom and skills in establishing comfortable and safe connections with others.

BOUNDARY CASTLE
EXERCISE INSTRUCTIONS

Although this illustration appears a little more complicated, it's actually quite simple. First of all, draw four rectangles to form a box as in Figure 5.1. Next, add the turrets on all four corners (see Figure 5.2). The turrets are the lookout towers from which the client will be able to evaluate the situation when people are approaching the castle wanting admittance. Some clients may not realize they have access to the turrets and will need to be shown the stairs.

The third step in this drawing is the drawbridge (see Figure 5.3). Typically, the damsel in distress has allowed the hinges to rust, making it difficult to raise or lower the drawbridge at will. He or she will need to identify and label the obstacles he or she encounters that keep him or her from oiling the drawbridge. The knight in shining armor, however, keeps the drawbridge well oiled.

The moat is the fourth step and forms an additional means of protection to keep out unwanted visitors (Figure 5.4). The therapist will

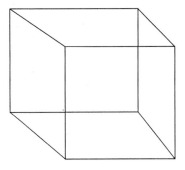

FIGURE 5.1. Draw a box.

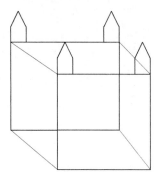

FIGURE 5.2. Add the turrets.

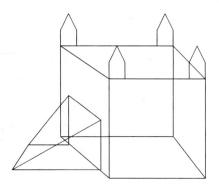

FIGURE 5.3. Include the drawbridge.

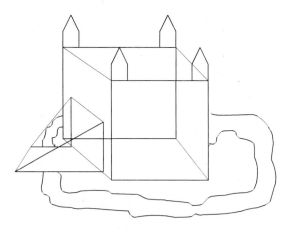

FIGURE 5.4. A moat will keep out unwanted visitors.

need to help the client analyze the effectiveness of the moat. If the water is too shallow, enemies will be able to approach the castle in spite of the moat. If the moat is too narrow, enemies could easily drop down a plank and walk right across.

The simple stick figure is now placed within the castle (Figure 5.5). After evaluation of the components of the castle, people will typically be able to recognize themselves as the damsel in distress or the knight in shining armor. The therapist will help the client identify his or her own unique qualities, which make up the character he or she has chosen. This might also be a good time to begin processing the client's life history and the circumstances that led to forming the role he or she is playing.

Finally, additional stick figures are drawn outside the castle walls (see Figure 5.6). They represent individuals who might want to approach and enter the castle. The therapist will help the client begin to analyze the situation and begin to teach him or her how to use the defenses that are at his or her disposal. The client will also learn when it's safe to let the drawbridge down and enjoy his or her guests.

VIGNETTE

Lisa, a twenty-two-year-old waitress, came to therapy because of continuing emotional problems following a rape in college. During

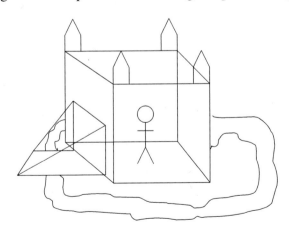

FIGURE 5.5. The client adds a stick figure to represent himself or herself.

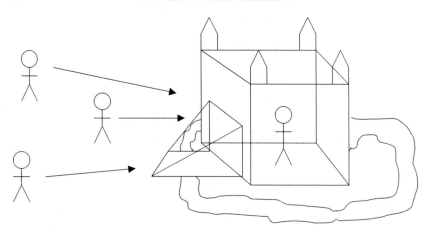

FIGURE 5.6. The additional people represent potential visitors, both positive and negative influences.

her freshman year, she had attended a sorority party, consumed more alcohol than she was used to, and had been taken advantage of by two young fraternity men invited to the party. These two young men were acquaintances of Lisa's best friend, Shelley, and she had trusted them to escort her back to her dorm when she realized she had drank too much to safely drive. Lisa had awakened alone in her room the next morning with her clothes torn and bruises on her arms and legs. She had few specific memories but deduced what had happened.

Lisa called her friend Shelley and told her what she suspected had happened. Shelley responded by saying she must have had a nightmare, and that these two young men were very popular in their fraternity and had good reputations. Lisa was still in a state of confusion and, without the support of her friend, felt she couldn't go through with reporting the incident to the police. She spent the next year trying to deny what happened but found that she was getting more and more depressed. Finally, unable to focus and keep up with her schoolwork, Lisa dropped out of college in her sophomore year. She got a job as a waitress but didn't know how much longer she could handle that either. She couldn't remember orders accurately and, occasionally, men would flirt with her and Lisa would begin shaking uncontrollably and have to leave work.

THERAPIST: Lisa, tell me what brings you here today.

LISA: I don't know how to begin. It's hard to think and I cry all the time. This has been going on for over two years now and I don't know how to stop.

THERAPIST: Lisa, did anything happen two years ago that may have started all this?

LISA: I think I was raped, but I'm not sure. My friend Shelley said it couldn't have happened, but I know something was wrong that night. I haven't been myself since. I really need some help because I can't go on like this.

Lisa burst into tears at this point and the therapist allowed her to cry for awhile. Once Lisa became more composed, the therapist evaluated her for depressive symptoms and discovered that she more than met the criteria for a major depression diagnosis. Lisa also revealed other symptoms she was struggling with, such as nightmares, hypervigilance, and social withdrawal. The initial recommendation by the therapist was for Lisa to see her primary care physician to be evaluated for medical management of her depressive symptoms. Lisa complied with taking her antidepressant medication and worked with the therapist on cognitive therapy targeting the depressive symptoms. She began experiencing significant relief within a few weeks.

THERAPIST: Lisa, I'm glad the depression has improved. However, I'm noticing as we talk how hard it is for you to say no to anyone, even when complying with their wishes is inconvenient for you. Has this always been the case?

LISA: Somewhat, though since the rape it's been impossible. I'm terrified of saying no and it feels like my "no" wouldn't be respected even if I did.

THERAPIST: That seems like an important issue to work on in order for you to regain your self-confidence in relationships. I think an illustration will help us work through this.

Lisa was willing to engage in this process and the therapist drew the castle.

THERAPIST: Lisa, most people have a defined, personal space over which they feel they have control. The castle walls represent the boundaries of that personal space. We also have certain defense mechanisms in place to protect ourselves when our castle walls feel threatened. The moat and the drawbridge represent the defenses we have at our disposal. Lisa, what defenses are you using to protect yourself?

LISA: None. I feel helpless and am terrified when anyone challenges my boundaries.

THERAPIST: So, it sounds like your drawbridge hinges are rusted and your moat is too shallow to be effective.

LISA: That's exactly what it feels like! Not only that, but it feels like the rape was an assault on my walls and they're crumbling.

THERAPIST: What an excellent analogy, Lisa. You're describing yourself as a damsel in distress, someone who feels inadequate to protect the personal space of her castle and is hoping against hope that a rescuer will come along. Rather than wait for a knight in shining armor to appear on a white horse, I would like to suggest that you might become the knight yourself.

LISA: That sounds great, but I have no idea how I would do that.

THERAPIST: Lisa, that is something we can work on together. This will take some time since knights train and prepare for a long while before they head out to do battle. Preparation and training will need to happen on two fronts. First of all, we will need to help you strengthen your inner self; second, we will need to help you be able to accurately evaluate any outside threats to your security.

Lisa did not venture outside her castle walls for quite some time. She still had multiple symptoms resulting from her earlier trauma and had much inner healing work to occupy her time and energy. The therapist worked with her on setting some basic limits so that she could raise her drawbridge and deepen her moat. Lisa desperately needed some safe space for her recovery. Once that work was well under way, Lisa and her therapist discovered the stairs to the turrets and she began her work on accurate recognition of any threats to her castle. She also learned to look for signs that those approaching her castle were safe and could be welcomed. Lisa began to experience a renewed sense of self-confidence and a new freedom in her interactions with others.

Diagnosis:	Major depression, single episode, severe without psychotic symptoms
	Post-traumatic stress disorder
Goals:	Resolution of her depressive symptoms
	Healing from past trauma
	Ability to set healthy boundaries around her personal space
	Improved self-confidence and self-esteem
Interventions:	Medication management for the depressive symptoms, which involved collaboration with her primary care physician
	Cognitive therapy to treat the depressive symptoms
	Processing of her past traumatic experience
	Assertiveness training
	Social skills training that focused on setting appropriate limits in different social situations

After several months of working on these difficult issues, Lisa became angry that the rape had caused her to discontinue her college education. She decided to use that anger in a positive way and re-enrolled in college. Lisa changed her major to criminal justice and vowed to use her experiences and insights to help others in similar situations. Although therapy had slowed down considerably by the time of her enrollment, she added some extra sessions as she faced the setting where her life had changed forever. The extra support was beneficial and Lisa was able to proceed on course to her goals.

SUGGESTIONS FOR FOLLOW-UP

The Boundary Castle illustration became a constant reminder and source of encouragement for Lisa. She made a few extra copies and kept one in her school notebook. It helped her remember what defenses she had and how to use them if needed. Periodically, Lisa came for booster therapy sessions. At times, certain situations or topics in her classes brought up painful memories for which she needed help to put in proper perspective.

Lisa had a relapse in her junior year when she saw the two men who had assaulted her at a college football game. She worked with her therapist on the recurrent trauma symptoms and also consulted an attorney to see what her legal options might be should she decide that course of action would be in her best interest. Lisa analyzed her Boundary Castle illustration once more and decided advanced self-defense training would strengthen her castle walls. She enrolled in a self-defense course especially designed for women who had been assaulted.

CONTRAINDICATIONS FOR USE

This illustration needs to carry the warning that the therapy needs to proceed in the proper order. The client who has difficulty monitoring and enforcing his or her personal space needs to fortify himself or herself on the inside before dealing with threats from without. To encourage engagement with the enemy before training and preparation is asking the client to commit emotional suicide. The client should be reassured that to withdraw from a threatening situation initially may be a wise tactical maneuver while he or she prepares and trains. This will build confidence and ensure a much greater chance of success.

This may not be an appropriate illustration to use with those clients who might be prone to violence. The vivid imagery of engaging in battle might feel like permission to engage in aggressive behavior for self-protection. This, of course, is not the message a therapist wants to communicate. As with any of the illustrations, the therapist must spend some time getting to know the client to know which illustration might best fit his or her needs.

Chapter 6

Well of Needs

OBJECTIVE

Having our emotional, psychological, spiritual, and physical needs met is essential for our overall well-being. Although no one person can meet all our needs, we expect some people to meet certain needs. For example, we expect parents to meet our physical and security needs during infancy. The Well of Needs illustration demonstrates what happens when our needs are not met in the expected manner, what happens when we get derailed in looking for other sources to meet our needs, and how to move in a healthy direction to have our needs met in legitimate ways.

RATIONALE

Human beings come into the world as helpless babies with many needs. Ideally, a baby is born into a family in which loving parents will meet his or her needs for security, food, shelter, clothing, and clean diapers in a timely and loving manner. As we grow, our needs become more complex and widespread. We have needs for friendship and socialization, needs for intellectual stimulation, needs for physical health, needs to explore spiritual issues, and needs for a sense of emotional well-being. People other than our parents play a part in meeting those needs. In addition, we have personal responsibilities to see that our needs are met.

Having unmet needs in our lives is like being thirsty for a drink of water. When we're thirsty, we instinctively go to "the source" to get a drink. For babies and young children, the source is typically their parents. Older children and adults might go to other family members,

Published by The Haworth Press, Inc., 2006. All rights reserved.
doi:10.1300/5397_06

teachers, spiritual leaders, friends, spouses, and so forth, depending on the nature of their needs. It is a healthy expectation that if we go to the appropriate individual and if we take on the appropriate personal responsibilities required by the situation, that our needs will be satisfactorily met. Of course, exceptions to this generalization exist. For example, we might go to a spouse to have our needs for affection met, but our spouse is trying to meet a deadline for work and is overwhelmed already by the expectations of his or her boss. However, as long as these situations are the exception rather than the norm, the temporary frustration we might experience in not having our needs met will be manageable.

In the Well of Needs illustration, the source is an old-fashioned well. A thirsty person will take the initiative to go to the well, lower a bucket into the well, and pull up the bucket of water to get a drink. This is a normal and reasonable process. However, at times the bucket is lowered into the well and comes to the surface filled with rocks rather than water. These are the times when the logical person to help with meeting our needs comes up short. This person either has nothing to give because his or her own resources are depleted or he or she chooses not to give what he or she has either out of ignorance, selfishness, a desire to punish, abusiveness, or a desire for vengeance.

Thirsty people who pull up rocks often continue to go back to the well for water because that's the logical place to go. After multiple instances of not having their thirst quenched, they may become dehydrated, so to speak, and become limited in their ability to think of other sources they might try in order to quench their thirst. Without water, their lives become a hot, dry desert. In desperation, they may try changing directions, heading out into the desert rather than going back to the well. However, it is quite easy to become enamored with a mirage. As we know, a mirage is only an illusion, although it may seem quite real for a time. Examples of mirages include dysfunctional relationships, chemical dependencies, workaholism, and so forth. A cycle may be established in which a person goes to the well for water, pulls up rocks, goes toward a mirage, experiences disappointments, and returns to the well to pull up more rocks. At this point, the dehydrated person might access therapy to help them find a drink of water.

The therapist then has the daunting task of helping the client recognize and understand why his or her particular well is full of rocks instead of water. If the client has been taken in by a mirage, the therapist will also need to help the client understand why the mirage didn't satisfy his or her thirst. Finally, the therapist has the treatment task of helping the client envision an oasis. The oasis represents healthy alternatives to the well that will quench the client's thirst. In order to find the oasis, the client will have to turn from the well into the desert, which may seem illogical to the client. The oasis may be behind sand dunes and difficult to see initially. Mirages will have to be identified and avoided. If the oasis is a considerable distance away, the client will need the therapist to come along as a guide and support. Helping the client to maintain the vision of the oasis can be challenging. The client might ask, "If I can't get water from a well, why should I believe that an oasis, which I can't even see, will supply the water I crave?" But how rewarding for the therapist who perseveres on the quest and has the privilege of seeing the client shout, "Eureka! There it is!"

WELL OF NEEDS
EXERCISE INSTRUCTIONS

The Well of Needs illustration obviously begins with drawing a person at the well, while at the same time explaining to the client how a well is the logical place to find a drink of water to quench one's thirst (see Figure 6.1). Next, it is explained that at times the well is dry

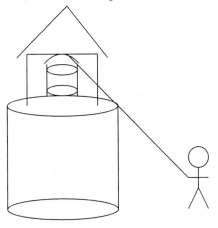

FIGURE 6.1. At the Well of Needs.

for various reasons, and the client may only get a bucket of rocks (as in Figure 6.2).

Once the rocks are drawn, it is helpful to have the client name the rocks. In other words, the client needs to begin to face the truth about his or her situation—namely, that the person who should be giving him or her a drink of refreshing and rejuvenating water is instead giving a toxic substitute (see Figure 6.3). If the client has tried to turn away from the well and satisfy his or her thirst through a mirage, it will also be important for them to recognize and acknowledge this (see Figure 6.4).

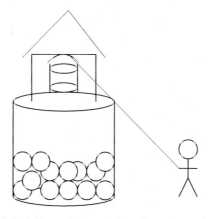

FIGURE 6.2. A dry well may yield only rocks and no water.

Criticism
Anger
Inconsistency
Rejection
Shame
Control
Selfishness
Humiliation

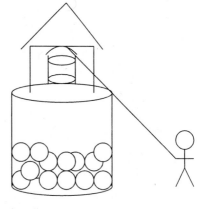

FIGURE 6.3. Have the client name the rocks.

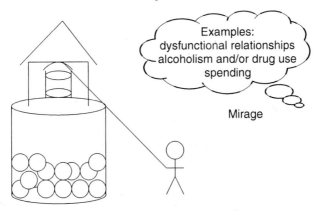

FIGURE 6.4. Mirages represent unhealthy and unsatisfying choices.

At this point, the client may need specific and specialized treatment for the "mirage" before they can continue. This might include treatment for drug and alcohol abuse, eating disorders, gambling addiction, and so forth. Grief work will also be important as the full impact of a dry well hits the client. The loss of a well that should have been full to overflowing plus the need to travel toward an oasis that may not yet be visible can be overwhelming to clients. As soon as possible, begin to help the client develop a vision of his or her oasis (see Figure 6.5).

Clients will need a lot of help, instruction, and encouragement to not only envision their oasis, but to make it a reality. The therapist will need to become the desert guide, helping the client to resist turning back to the well, helping them to avoid turning to mirages, and helping them to keep the goal in sight.

VIGNETTE

Andrea was a thirty-two-year-old woman who attend therapy sessions because of depressive symptoms. She couldn't sleep, had lost her appetite along with twenty pounds in the past month, and had no energy or motivation to go on with her life. In fact, she had been having suicidal thoughts on an increasing basis and she was frightened. During the initial interview, the therapist noted that Andrea hesitated

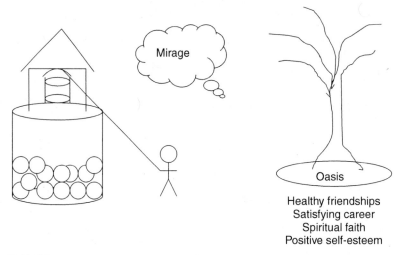

Mirage

Oasis

Healthy friendships
Satisfying career
Spiritual faith
Positive self-esteem

FIGURE 6.5. Developing an oasis can give the client a goal to work toward.

and was reluctant to talk about her support system. The therapist in-
formed Andrea that with her presenting symptoms, a support system
would be very important for her safety and eventual recovery. Andrea
began crying and, in a frustrated voice, stated, "If I could count on my
family, why do you think I'd be here?"

By the end of the interview, the therapist had uncovered feelings of
deep unhappiness in Andrea regarding her family connections. According to Andrea, her father was an alcoholic and her mother the
poster child for enablers. She had an older brother who had dropped
out of high school at sixteen and was now in prison after robbing a
convenience store. Andrea spoke of her attempts to get support from
her parents for her depression and their response of "Life is tough.
Get a grip." Initially, the therapist instructed Andrea to immediately
see her family physician for a medication evaluation and also had her
sign a no-suicide contract. Andrea agreed to the plan and indeed followed through with the suggestions. Within a few weeks she began
feeling better and came to therapy with an apology.

ANDREA: Dr. S., thank you so much for your help. I remember I was
   quite rude to you in our first session when you asked me about my
   family and I want to apologize.

THERAPIST: Andrea, that's quite all right. But your reaction did suggest that there may be significant problems in your relationship with your family. Would you like to talk about that?

ANDREA: I wouldn't like to, but I know I need to. They've never been there for me and whenever I ask them for help with anything, I'm always disappointed.

The therapist asked Andrea to describe her family in detail along with typical interactions between them. Her father, an alcoholic, seldom worked and was a demanding, self-centered man who seemed to have little love or tolerance for his two children. He had been physically abusive to them at times and when Andrea was nine years old, the Department of Social Services had been called by the school when they saw bruises on Andrea's arm. She and her brother had spent six months in a foster home before returning to their parents. Andrea's brother was very angry over this and never forgave her. Her mother, a passive woman who worked menial jobs to help support the family, was also angry at Andrea for what happened. As a classic enabler, Andrea's mother spent her life trying to cover up her husband's faults.

THERAPIST: Andrea, I would like to use an illustration to help us better understand your family dynamics and the impact that has had on you.

Andrea agreed and the therapist explained that our emotional, physical, and psychological needs can feel like being thirsty for a cool glass of water. She explained that it is a logical assumption that one should be able to go to a well and pull up a bucket of cool water to quench that thirst.

THERAPIST: But Andrea, it seems that instead of water, each time you go to the well, you pull up a bucket of rocks instead. And, based on your history, you've gone back to the well many times without ever experiencing any success.

ANDREA: You're right. I got a few drops of water the time I had my appendix removed, but it only made me long for more and it just wasn't there.

THERAPIST: If you had to name the rocks, what would they be called? In other words, what *do* you get when you go to the well?

ANDREA: That's not a hard question. I get anger, criticism, abuse, blame, and disrespect.

THERAPIST: What keeps you going back?

ANDREA: I don't know where else to go. Besides, I would feel so guilty if I turned my back on my family. I know what they are, but they're my family and surely they deserve some loyalty on my part. What if they changed and I wasn't there? I couldn't live with myself if I just abandoned them.

THERAPIST: Then I have two questions for you. How long have you pulled the same rocks up in your bucket? And what evidence do you have that it will be different next time?

ANDREA: I get the point. And there is no evidence. I have to admit that the only evidence that's there indicates that the next bucket will also be full of rocks. Actually, I have tried getting away, but it was worse than my family.

THERAPIST: What did you try, Andrea?

ANDREA: Well, when I was eighteen, I got married. But I got pregnant right away and Ed got angry. He said that wasn't the plan and he ended up beating me so badly, I lost the baby. I've never gotten over that. Eventually I divorced him but I feel like I've been paying for that attempt to escape ever since.

The therapist explained mirages to Andrea and how they initially seem to be the answer to all of our problems. But the illusion evaporates quickly, often leaving us in worse shape than we were in before. It was obvious to the therapist that Andrea's self-esteem had suffered greatly from her life experiences and that she had little confidence to begin a trek through the desert to try to find an oasis. The therapist worked with Andrea to help her develop more ego strength over the next several weeks before introducing her to the concept of the oasis.

ANDREA: An oasis! Why didn't you tell me about this before?

THERAPIST: It didn't seem that you were ready. It is very difficult to turn your back on all you've known to head toward a desert with no oasis in sight. But it's time to begin developing that vision. Go to your imagination and try to envision what your oasis would look like.

ANDREA: I want so much to have a husband and children where we are truly loving toward one another. In other words, a family the opposite of what I've had. I would also like to be stronger within myself, confident that I can make healthy choices for my life.

THERAPIST: Those are great goals, Andrea. I will be your guide as you begin this journey across the desert.

Diagnosis:	Major depression, single episode, severe, without psychotic features
	Passive personality
Goals:	Resolution of depressive symptoms
	Develop the ability to interact in a healthy manner in relationships
	Develop positive self-esteem and self-confidence in her strengths
Interventions:	Collaboration with family physician to treat depressive symptoms
	Exploration of family-of-origin issues
	Grief therapy to help her accept the losses she'd experienced in her life
	Assertiveness training
	Social skills training

Andrea hadn't anticipated how difficult this journey would be and was glad that she had developed a solid relationship with her therapist prior to beginning. She struggled with grief, with feelings of selfishness for focusing on her own needs, and with guilt for saying "no more" to the rocks. Andrea made it to her oasis in time. She met a nice man through her workplace and developed a loving relationship that eventually welcomed two children. Andrea wanted to make sure that she was a well full of water for her own husband and children. Therefore, she periodically came back to therapy for checkups to make sure she was not being enticed by mirages or failing to supply water to her family through ignorance.

SUGGESTIONS FOR FOLLOW-UP

The Well of Needs illustration was shocking to Andrea at first as she realized how emotionally dehydrated she had become. She needed much support and encouragement as she began to consider turning away from the empty well. The only time she had tried that on her own had been disastrous and she therefore had no self-confidence to try again. It was essential that Andrea begin to develop other sources to obtain water outside her family. A grief support group was recommended even though Andrea's losses weren't as immediately tangible as those of others in the group. She eventually tried other social groups and sought out her therapist frequently to assess her responses. These visits became less and less frequent as Andrea began to develop self-confidence.

She and her husband attended therapy sessions together when the relationship became serious. The therapist helped them both to understand what a healthy marital relationship would look like and they worked together to discover appropriate ways to get emotional needs met. Again, when Andrea had children, some of her old reactions of insecurity returned. She was terrified of repeating her parents' mistakes. Her therapist directed her to a good parenting group from which she could learn effective parenting skills and also receive support as a new and inexperienced mother.

CONTRAINDICATIONS FOR USE

The Well of Needs illustration represents clinical issues that are often deep and have a long history. Therefore, working through the Well of Needs illustration should not be rushed. The recognition of deep losses and inadequacies can be devastating and the client should be allowed adequate time to go through a grieving experience that might be quite intense. If a client has become involved in mirages as a means of trying to find water, serious consequences may have to be dealt with in order to stabilize the client before pushing on to further growth.

A solid, trusting relationship with the therapist will be essential prior to heading across the desert toward the oasis. If the journey is suggested and encouraged before the development of this therapeutic alliance, failure and/or discouragement is very possible. It is often just too frightening to begin a lengthy journey to an unknown destination alone. The client will need to collect resources, equipment, and some experience before commencing on this journey and they will need time and direction to help them do that task. To send a client into the desert without proper equipment and skills may lead to failure and the refusal of the client to ever want to try again. This is likely to be a long-term journey. The therapist and client should recognize this fact and be as committed as possible to seeing the journey through to the destination.

Chapter 7

Weight of the World

OBJECTIVE

The Weight of the World illustration serves to demonstrate the cumulative effect that stressors can have in our lives. As each stressor is dealt with and removed from the load on the client, the Weight of the World illustration helps the client visually experience relief as he or she sees the load lighten.

RATIONALE

A certain amount of stress is normal and even positive in our lives. Stress can motivate and challenge us to achieve meaningful goals. Without stress, we might not want to go to work, exercise, fix meals, or invest in quality relationships. However, when stress reaches levels where performance and motivation begin to decrease, problems arise. No one would argue that excessive stress can damage our physical and emotional health. Sometimes stressful situations come upon us all at once, as in the cases of loss of a job, death of a loved one, or a car accident. Those stressors are so significant that we recognize them immediately and must take steps to manage the crisis.

However, sometimes stressors sneak up on us and we don't recognize how they've accumulated until we begin to break down. Our bodies have been created to handle short-term stress very efficiently. Our adrenaline levels rise to the occasion, we contain the situation, and then we must rest and allow our bodies to recuperate before tackling the next stressful situation. If the stressor(s) remain and we're forced to continue trying to manage the stress, we must make adjustments. Those adjustments may include denial, minimization, neglect

Published by The Haworth Press, Inc., 2006. All rights reserved.
doi:10.1300/5397_07

of other commitments, and so forth. Over time, we assimilate the higher level of stress into our everyday lives and may ignore the negative effects we begin to experience. Since our bodies do not handle this type of long-term stress efficiently, it will eventually become exhausted with deleterious physical and emotional effects that we can no longer deny. Examples of this type of long-term stress include an unhappy marriage, a boss we can't please, a thirty-year mortgage that is slightly beyond our reach, chronic health problems, etc.

This type of consistent, long-term stress can act as a heavy weight on a person's shoulders. The Weight of the World illustration demonstrates this in a very visual manner. Have you ever held your arms out at shoulder level and tried to maintain that position? It's fairly easy for a short period of time. But have you tried to hold that position for an indefinite length of time? Even without additional weight on your arms, it becomes impossible after awhile. Just sustaining the weight of our arms alone becomes more than we're able to manage over time. Of course, some people are in better physical condition than others and can hold the position longer.

Stress can feel similar to physical weights. Again, some people are in better emotional shape than others and can handle stress effectively for longer periods of time. However, all of us have our limits. Imagine how you feel when you've reached the limits of what you can manage and still know you have to hang on. It's unbearable. Then imagine the relief you experience when the weight of the stress is removed, one piece at a time. The Weight of the World illustration helps clients to clearly visualize the load they've been carrying and to visually experience the relief of having their load lightened.

WEIGHT OF THE WORLD
EXERCISE INSTRUCTIONS

The Weight of the World illustration is one of the easiest illustrations to draw, but don't underestimate the impact it can have on clients. The first step is, once again, drawing the basic stick figure. This time, however, the figure has extraordinarily long arms to hold the bricks of stress (see Figure 7.1). The next step is to draw a load of bricks on the arms of the stick figure. Each brick represents one stressor the client may be trying to manage (see Figure 7.2).

FIGURE 7.1. Figure with very long arms.

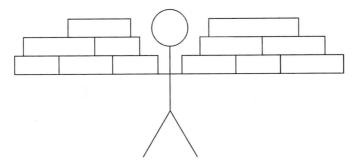

FIGURE 7.2. Each arm holds many bricks.

The final step is having the client identify the stressors in their lives and label each brick. Draw one brick for each identified stressor in the client's life (see Figure 7.3 for an example). After each stressor is examined and therapeutic intervention has provided the client with relief, use the Weight of the World illustration to help the client visualize his or her lightened load (see Figure 7.4 as an example).

VIGNETTE

David came to therapy with complaints of anxiety and panic attacks. He described the following symptoms: insomnia, poor appetite, hand tremors, poor concentration and memory, and increased heart rate with occasional shortness of breath. David reported that

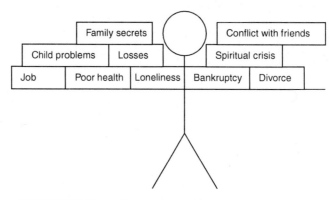

FIGURE 7.3. Example stressors that a person might carry.

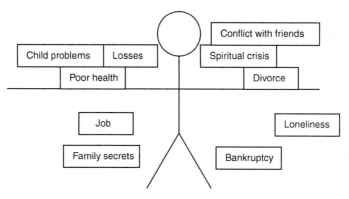

FIGURE 7.4. The client must allow some of these stressors to fall away.

he had been experiencing some of the symptoms for the past six months, but they had been increasing within the past month and it was getting difficult to go to work. Being around other people, including family members and co-workers, was also becoming increasingly difficult. David had been concerned about the physical symptoms and had already visited his family physician. His physician had recommended a short leave of absence from work, started him on some medication to treat the anxiety symptoms, and recommended he begin therapy as well.

David was obviously nervous and anxious during his first therapy session, fidgeting in his chair, avoiding direct eye contact, speaking with hesitancy and a tremor in his voice, and exhibiting sweaty palms. As the therapist eased into assessing the problem, David began to reveal a history of steadily escalating stressors in his life. He had married young after only one year of college. He loved his wife and didn't regret their decision, but it had been difficult to find a good-paying job. Now, at age twenty-eight, David had just found out that his wife was expecting their first child. Although they had planned on having children at some point, this was earlier than they had anticipated. David had always wanted to finish his education and had been taking some evening classes to begin achieving that goal.

Neither David nor his wife, Bridget, had supportive relationships with their extended families. They had always felt they were on their own to manage problems. Both were hardworking individuals, but they also indulged themselves with "toys," which they felt they deserved. David had just purchased a new sports car when Bridget began having complications with the pregnancy and had to quit her job in her fifth month. David was now confronted with unexpected medical bills in addition to a large car payment. He had taken on a second part-time job three months before starting therapy. Now he was afraid of losing both jobs.

THERAPIST: David, it seems that a number of problems and responsibilities have been piling up over the past few months. What have you been doing to take care of yourself?

DAVID: I'm just trying to survive. I get up, go to work, come home for dinner and check on Bridget, then go to work or class again. I'm lucky if I get six hours of sleep each night. Right now, my responsibility is to take care of Bridget and the baby.

THERAPIST: Well, that's admirable, but it seems to be costing you a lot in terms of your health.

DAVID: Tell me about it. I don't know what I'll do if I lose my jobs.

THERAPIST: I'd like to use an illustration to take a look at all the things you're dealing with right now.

DAVID: Sure, if you think that will help.

The therapist drew the stick figure (which got a chuckle from David) and then began to draw the bricks on the figure's arms. She asked David to begin labeling each brick with a stressor he was experiencing (see Figure 7.5).

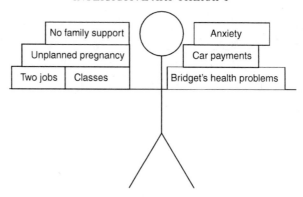

FIGURE 7.5. David's stressors.

DAVID: Stop! I can't hold anymore, my arms will fall off. And, I can tell you, you don't know the half of it. What do I do?

THERAPIST: It looks heavy to me as well. It seems that we need to develop a plan in therapy to help you begin to unload some of those bricks.

DAVID: I can't wait. No wonder I was feeling so burdened. I never realized how much was getting piled on.

David and the therapist took a close look at each brick; first, to try to determine why it was there in the first place, and second, to see if it could be dropped or modified to ease the weight.

DAVID: Well, the most obvious thing I should get rid of is the new car. It's just that growing up, my family never had much money and I was always told I wouldn't amount to anything. I felt I wanted to prove them all wrong and I also wanted the "cool" toy I never had.

THERAPIST: That's an important insight and I think it would be helpful to examine why you felt such a strong need to gain your family's approval in light of their poor treatment of you.

DAVID: I can't do anything about the baby and, frankly speaking, I wouldn't want to. This baby is already loved and a blessing to Bridget and me.

THERAPIST: I totally understand. But the pregnancy complications are a strain on both of you. Being knowledgeable about what's going on physiologically would likely help ease some of the stress.

At least you would know what you might expect and be able to prepare yourselves to handle things. Also, make sure you get counseling from your obstetrician about protective and strengthening
measures you and Bridget could take. These things won't remove
the brick, but they can make it smaller.

David and the therapist went through each brick in the same manner. In order for David to begin experiencing some immediate relief
from his anxiety and panic symptoms, they discussed the bricks
quickly at first. They wanted to discover if any of the bricks could be
removed quickly and easily. David hadn't owned his car for long and
was able to go back to the dealer and trade it in for something more af-
fordable. He and Bridget found out through their obstetrician about a
support group for people experiencing high-risk pregnancies. They
immediately joined. Those two things alone helped relieve enough of
David's stress that he began to worry less about losing his jobs.

Diagnosis:	Anxiety disorder
	Panic disorder without agoraphobia
Goals:	Reduction of stress
	Develop the ability to manage stress successfully
	Exploration and resolution, if possible, of family-of-origin issues
Interventions:	Relaxation exercises
	Stress-management techniques
	Exploration and processing of family-of-origin issues
	Development of community resources
	Medication management by David's family physician

David learned and faithfully practiced the relaxation techniques
his therapist taught him. He also experienced improvement from the
medications his physician had prescribed. As David became calmer
and more in control of his emotions, Bridget began to relax as well.
Some of her negative symptoms began to dissipate and both of them
began to enjoy the pregnancy once again. At this point, the therapist
revisited each brick with David, helping him examine why the bricks

had accumulated in the first place and what he could do to prevent them from piling up again.

SUGGESTIONS FOR FOLLOW-UP

It is almost inevitable that clients will feel overwhelmed the first time they see the reality of the heavy load they're carrying in a pictorial manner. This is one time when weight-lifting exercises are *not* beneficial to your health! If it's reasonable, help clients to unload as many bricks as possible right away. Once they feel less burdened, they will be encouraged to continue. The therapist can then help clients examine the makeup of each brick, determining why the brick is so heavy. This is how the therapist approached the situation with David.

It is important to keep the Weight of the World illustration available for future reference. Carrying around such a large load of bricks has built some muscle, and clients may feel they can add additional bricks once they've experienced a lighter load. In fact, they might fear getting weak if they don't continue to exercise those muscles with extra responsibilities! Clients can be reminded of their discomfort and oppression by reexamining their original illustrations. They can also be reminded of the relief they felt when they saw the bricks fall to the floor.

CONTRAINDICATIONS FOR USE

It is important for clients to have the right tools in place before removing their load of bricks. They will need supports under their arms to avoid injury as they dismantle the burden they're carrying. The right tools might include stress-management skills, medication management, support groups, and so forth. Clients will also need to be willing to reexamine their views of emotional and mental health. If they persist in believing that the stronger person is the one who can carry the heavier load, they are doomed to a breakdown. Therapists will need to be alert to the core beliefs behind the accumulation of bricks.

Chapter 8

Swamp of Sympathy

OBJECTIVE

The purpose of the Swamp of Sympathy illustration is to demonstrate the significant differences between sympathy and empathy. Many individuals have mistakenly thought of these two concepts as one and the same, to the detriment of their relationships. In understanding these two different concepts, people can begin to make clear choices about what behaviors are most helpful in relationships with others in need.

RATIONALE

Most people truly desire to be helpful and giving to friends, family, and even strangers who are less fortunate. We all, at one time or another, come across situations or individuals that tug at our heartstrings. If we allow our hearts to completely rule how we help others, we can easily get into situations where we become emotionally drained—and possibly drained of physical resources as well. People may intentionally or unintentionally take advantage of our soft hearts and discomfort with suffering. It would be tragic if we lost that sensitivity to others' needs.

The problem is that each of us has our own needs as well. If these needs are ignored, we become the ones suffering. Besides having our own needs, we also have limited resources. Resources include time, money, physical strength and stamina, emotional strength and stamina, and so forth. Once these resources are depleted, we have nothing left to give to others except "I wish I could help." We may even become

Published by The Haworth Press, Inc., 2006. All rights reserved.
doi:10.1300/5397_08

angry and bitter that others have taken or used all we have and may have given us little to nothing in return.

Balance is the key to this situation, but it can be very difficult to maintain or even understand. Airline safety instructions provide a great example of maintaining a healthy balance with those in need. Think of how the flight attendant discusses how to use the oxygen mask. The instructions primarily refer to parents and children but could apply to anyone nearby who is weaker in some way. The "parents" are instructed to apply the oxygen masks first so they can remain conscious and able to help their "children." Our resources must be replenished on a consistent basis in order to be able to give to others. In the airplane example, the resource is oxygen. Other examples might include going to work to replenish financial resources, exercising to replenish our mental clarity and maintain our physical health, or even time alone to replenish spiritual and emotional resources.

Guilt often enters the picture when we try to take care of our resources. Others might accuse us of selfishness if we're not "helping out" as much or as often as they deem necessary. Guilt can lead to ignoring our own needs and allowing our resources to disappear. "No," "not now," or "I can't" may be the most difficult words to utter in situations in which the needs of others are so great. If saying these words leads to excessive guilt, we may allow that guilt to drive us into a state of complete exhaustion. In this case, we run the danger of drowning along with the ones we were trying to help.

The Swamp of Sympathy illustration clearly demonstrates this concept. The swamp represents the mire of problems that we experience throughout our lives. Sometimes people fight their problems through denial, anger, dependency, rebellion, and so forth, rather than by engaging in effective problem solving. We've likely seen enough television scenes to visualize that when a person fights the swamp, they tend to sink even faster, eventually drowning. Sympathy is when we see people struggling in the swamp and feel so bad about their circumstances that we dive right in to be with them in their misery. The intent, wanting to be supportive and comforting, is often quite noble. However, the likely result is that we drown together.

Empathy also involves recognizing that people in the swamp are experiencing serious and possibly life-threatening circumstances. The difference is that empathic people remain on solid ground and make every attempt to remain objective. They assess the drowning person's situation, noting what remaining resources the drowning person might still possess and his or her capability of drawing upon those resources. They also assess their own store of resources and determine what they can realistically offer without excessively depleting their own resources.

Although this might sound very sterile, it's only part of the empathic person's response. Empathic people also genuinely try to imagine the feelings the drowning person might be experiencing and what it would be like to be in that swamp. They may be mistaken as cold-hearted, insensitive, or self-centered when they don't dive in, but this isn't the case. They have the wisdom to understand that two people drowning accomplishes nothing. Once empathic people have objectively determined to the best of their ability what might be helpful and how much they can reasonably contribute, they remain on solid ground and hold out a log to the drowning person. The drowning person is instructed and encouraged from solid ground how to grab onto the log in order to be pulled to land.

SWAMP OF SYMPATHY
EXERCISE INSTRUCTIONS

This is another very easy illustration to draw, but one that is quite powerful in helping clients gain insight into giving and receiving help in relationships. The first step, of course, is to draw the swamp and the drowning person, as in Figure 8.1. Since the swamp represents this individual's problems, have the client identify them as specifically as possible (Figure 8.2). The client might be the person in the

FIGURE 8.1. The basic drawing of a swamp and a drowning person.

swamp, wondering how to obtain help from others in a healthy manner or wondering why he or she isn't getting the help he or she needs. Allow the situation to guide the approach.

Next, draw a picture of solid ground with a tree. Also draw another stick figure near the tree (see Figure 8.3). The tree represents resources and will supply the log needed for the empathic person to help the individual in the swamp. Now help the person on solid ground identify his or her available resources and also to assess the situation of the person in the swamp (see Figure 8.4).

Finally, assist the client in choosing the log he or she is going to use to help the person in the swamp. The log represents what available resources will provide the best possible outcome for the rescue (see Figure 8.5). For example, suppose the person in the swamp is overwhelmed with debt and the person on solid ground is a professional

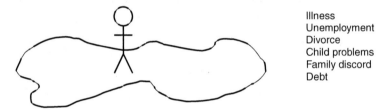

Illness
Unemployment
Divorce
Child problems
Family discord
Debt

FIGURE 8.2. List the problems the client is experiencing.

FIGURE 8.3. Solid ground and a tree represent resources.

Problems	Resources
Illness	Savings
Unemployment	Time available
Divorce	Knowledge
Child problems	Energy level
Family discord	Skills
Debt	Family support

FIGURE 8.4. List resources available to help reduce the problems.

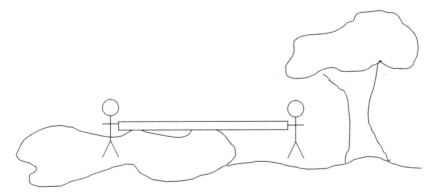

FIGURE 8.5. Choosing the right size log (resources) will help the individual escape from the swamp.

accountant. The accountant would need to determine if his or her particular skills are suitable for the situation, if he or she has the time to devote to helping, and if his or her family will be supportive of his or her time away from home while helping.

VIGNETTE

Kate was at her wit's end. Her daughter, Amy, was now thirteen, and everything seemed to be going wrong. At first, Kate had attributed the problems to Amy's becoming a teenager. "You know how teens are!" she kept saying. But Amy's behavior had gotten so out of hand that Kate felt she could no longer keep the family going on her own. She knew that she had spoiled Amy, but she had so loved being a mother, it had been a pleasure. Until now, that is. Amy's demands, as well as her tantrums if her demands weren't met, had escalated. She wanted a new computer for her room, unlimited access to the Internet, no curfew, the latest clothing styles, and taxi service on demand. And, oh, lest we forget, *no* chores around the house. Kate had begun to realize that she should have been setting limits on Amy's behavior all along. She had recently tried to enforce a curfew and discovered that Amy had just slipped out her bedroom window and gone where she wanted anyway.

Kate's husband, Jim, had given up long ago, blaming Kate's permissive style on all the family problems they were experiencing now. Credit card bills were mounting as Kate tried to pacify Amy out of tantrums that were now becoming more aggressive and violent. Amy had slammed her door shut and broken the lock. When Kate tried to get her to do chores to pay for the repairs, Amy began screaming so loud, Kate was afraid the neighbors would call the police. She gave in and fixed it herself. Another issue was Amy's deteriorating grades at school. She had also received some detentions for getting into fights with other kids. Kate was becoming exhausted from trying to work some overtime to catch up on the credit card debt, staying up late to help Amy with her homework, and then taking Amy and her friends wherever they wanted to go on weekends.

THERAPIST: Kate, you look and sound exhausted.

KATE: I am. And worried. This stress with Amy has put such a strain on my marriage that Jim threatened to separate if I didn't get help. All I ever wanted was to show Amy how much I loved her and it's all backfired! Jim is right; I have always given in to Amy and she hasn't learned to appreciate anything I do for her. Last week, I told her she couldn't go to a sleepover with her friends because she got an F on her math test. She went to her room and slammed the door.

The next morning when she came downstairs, she had cuts all over her arms. I was so upset. Then Amy threw it back in my face, saying I was to blame for not letting her go out. Amy's in trouble, too, and just won't admit it. What can I do?

THERAPIST: Let's use an illustration to help us look at your situation. Both you and Amy are struggling. It sounds like she has some serious problems right now and that you're overwhelmed by trying to help her. At the same time, you sincerely love your daughter and want to be able to communicate that to her. Imagine, if you will, that Amy is walking through a swamp and is getting sucked into some quicksand.

KATE: That's not much of a stretch for my imagination. That's exactly how it feels.

THERAPIST: You are standing on the ground and have started to go into the swamp to help rescue Amy. As you hold your arm out to help pull Amy back to solid ground, she is fighting you rather than allowing you to help pull her out. Now you're at the place where you feel that the quicksand in the swamp is beginning to pull you under also. Does that feel like an accurate description?

KATE: I couldn't have said it better. What do I do before we both go completely under?

This question of Kate's spurred a discussion of the difference between sympathy and empathy. Kate recognized that she had felt sorry for Amy because she was an only child. Kate herself had been an only child of low-income parents. She had been teased at school because of her out-of-date clothes, and had no siblings at home to commiserate with her. When she and Jim had married, she had vowed that her children would not have to repeat her own unhappy childhood. Unfortunately, she and Jim were not able to have other children after Amy. Kate was determined that Amy would at least have all the material possessions and privileges that she had been denied. Jim had a good job and Kate also worked very hard to provide extras.

Now Kate realized that she had been feeling sorry for Amy because of her own unresolved childhood unhappiness. She also recognized that Amy had learned to manipulate her through guilt. Kate accepted the guilty feelings easily and admitted that she was partly in denial that Amy was so manipulative and uncaring toward her. Kate had become desperate to turn the situation around and had indeed stepped into the swamp to try to reclaim Amy.

THERAPIST: Kate, in order to become an empathic helper, you are going to have to back out of the swamp and remain on solid ground no matter how much pressure Amy might place on you to join her in the quicksand. Your own emotions might work against you in that endeavor, but we can work through that together if you're willing.

KATE: Absolutely. I know that if I don't do this, I will lose Amy, Jim, and myself. I suppose Amy might still drown if she continues to fight me, and unfortunately, I predict that will happen. But at least this way, I will have a better chance to help her and I can also work on reclaiming my marriage.

THERAPIST: Okay. We're on our way. First, we must identify Amy's problems so that we can match appropriate resources to try to help her. Strengthening your empathy skills will be very helpful with this process. Empathy means that we will try the best we can to put ourselves in Amy's place and imagine what she must be going through, while at the same time remaining on firm ground.

(See Figure 8.6.)

THERAPIST: Kate, this is a beginning list. Since Amy hasn't been communicating well with you, she may have other problems of which you aren't yet aware. And you may have resources you haven't yet tapped into. We can add to both lists as we go along. Next we will need to hold out to Amy a log of genuine help. An obvious place to begin is to match your health insurance resources to Amy's need for therapy. I can suggest an excellent therapist who has experience working with troubled adolescents if you like.

KATE: That sounds like an excellent idea. Do you know anyone who could provide marital therapy for Jim and me? I really believe that with some help, we can recapture the closeness we once enjoyed. I know I can't manage the problems with Amy without his help.

THERAPIST: Absolutely. I'll give you the names of both therapists before you leave. Now, let's begin our work today with helping you to remain on solid ground even though Amy will likely try to pull you into the swamp.

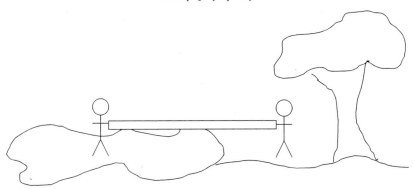

Amy's problems	*Kate's resources*
Failing in school	Life experience
Cutting behavior	Solid finances
Defiance of authority	Health insurance
Few self-help skills	Love for Amy
Family discord	Jim

FIGURE 8.6. Kate's swamp illustration.

Diagnosis:	Parent-child relational problem
	Partner relational problem
Goals:	Marital satisfaction
	A positive relationship with her daughter, Amy
	Resolution of her own childhood issues
	The ability to discipline Amy in a positive manner
	The acquisition of well-grounded parenting skills
Interventions:	Exploration of childhood issues
	Parenting-skills training
	Marital therapy
	Family therapy when Amy was willing to partici-pate
	Self-help skills training

The therapist and Kate continued their work, helping Kate learn to set appropriate boundaries with Amy. They also worked on helping Kate engage in positive self-care activities, as her own strength was almost depleted. As Jim saw how hard Kate was working on making these positive changes in her life, he became her most ardent supporter. Jim also had some good ideas on how to help with Amy. He had felt undermined when Kate was being so permissive and indulgent. Of course, Amy was fighting all these changes in her life. She did agree to meet with a therapist, however, and acknowledged privately in her own sessions that she was struggling and would like the situation to be different. This was a start, and Kate felt the prognosis for her family was better than it had ever been.

SUGGESTIONS FOR FOLLOW-UP

The Swamp of Sympathy illustration was added to many times during the course of therapy. Kate indeed had many internal resources that she hadn't initially recognized. For one thing, she learned that her difficult childhood had actually helped her acquire some insights into Amy's peer relationships and some strengths in standing up for herself. The log was whittled over time to become an effective tool in helping Amy out of the swamp, matching problems with appropriate resources. She also drew Jim (stick figure, of course) standing beside her on the solid ground, helping her hold the log out for Amy.

In time, when Amy was in a healthier emotional state and participating in family therapy with her parents, Kate decided it would be helpful to share the Swamp of Sympathy illustration with her. Amy could then see the process her mother had gone through to help her. She gained a better understanding of why her mother's behavior toward her had changed. As Amy matured, it made sense, and she began to appreciate how difficult it had been for her mother to pull out of the swamp and work to remain on solid ground. The illustration became a bond between them as they continued to work on having a close, healthy relationship.

CONTRAINDICATIONS FOR USE

Sympathy and empathy are more abstract concepts than some of the other illustrations demonstrate. Therefore, clients working on this illustration will need to have the cognitive ability to grasp the abstract thinking required for clear visualization. Otherwise, the process will be nothing less than frustrating and confusing. Also, some clients will have precious few resources to help them stay on solid ground. These clients might need some remedial work on development of personal resources before they feel equipped to handle the concepts involved in the Swamp of Sympathy illustration.

Chapter 9

Brick Wall of Barriers

OBJECTIVE

Most people have goals that they dream of achieving. Sometimes, we get to a place in our lives when we recognize that these goals haven't been met. The Brick Wall of Barriers illustration helps us picture barriers that may have interfered with reaching the goals we've dreamed about. As the bricks that make up the barrier are knocked away, people will be able to clearly see the way to experiencing the reality of these goals.

RATIONALE

Goals are the things that keep us future oriented. They provide the motivation we need to learn new skills, establish new relationships, and take healthy new risks. Working toward meaningful goals provides us with the thrill of achievements and a sense of accomplishment. We gain self-satisfaction and the realization that we've made a difference in the world. Our goals may place us in competition with others who have similar goals. If this is a healthy competition, it propels us onward to reach our prize. Having positive goals to work toward keeps us mentally alert and emotionally sound.

If we haven't taken the time to establish positive goals for our lives or if we lose sight of the ones we've had, negative changes begin to take place. It becomes difficult to motivate ourselves to go to work every day. We may begin to feel drained of energy. Relationships may

Published by The Haworth Press, Inc., 2006. All rights reserved.
doi:10.1300/5397_09

be avoided as we see others moving past us on the way to their own goals. Our self-esteem and sense of self-worth may plummet. Depression is a common occurrence for those with no goals. Some may go so far as to think they have no purpose for living. Discouragement sets in and we may get no farther than the couch when we get up in the morning.

The barriers that keep us from reaching our goals may be erected spontaneously through no fault of our own, or we may take on the construction ourselves. The identity of the architect is therefore an important truth to uncover. Barriers erected by others may or may not be easily overcome. However, it is somehow more bearable if we can recognize that the barriers may be beyond our control. If we erect our own barriers that prevent us from reaching our goals, often more is at stake. The barriers may represent a personal failure or inadequacy that can be difficult to accept.

Some barriers may be vague or even invisible. People may consistently work hard and never achieve their goals. The reasons why may be evasive and tough to pin down. We all can be blind to aspects of ourselves that are obvious to others but of which we ourselves are unaware. For example, an individual may live in a working-class neighborhood and dream of a college education to prepare him or her for a career in medicine, enabling him or her to move to the suburbs and have a better life. The person works very hard and makes the grades to earn a full scholarship to an Ivy League college. Although this person may have been popular and well-liked in his or her hometown, he or she can't seem to make friends in college. This person may be unaware that the social rules for fitting in are different in the Ivy League environment. However, this barrier is quite real, although invisible to our upward climber.

The Brick Wall of Barriers will help the client clearly identify those items that are keeping him or her from reaching goals. By tackling one brick at a time, the task of tearing down the wall doesn't seem so daunting. The time and effort it takes to do this will, of course, depend on how high the wall has been constructed. Once enough of the wall has come down so that the client can begin to peek over the top and again know that the goals remain, he or she will be motivated to continue.

BRICK WALL OF BARRIERS
EXERCISE INSTRUCTIONS

Straight lines and a stick figure are all that's required for this illustration. The first step is to draw the stick figure and, as much as possible, help the client to identify goals he or she has had or would like to have (see Figure 9.1). The next step is to draw the brick barrier that prevents the client from reaching his or her goals. Each brick is identified as specifically as possible (see Figure 9.2). Each barrier is examined in detail, discussing its impact on goals, assessing what would need to happen to knock the brick out of the wall, what it would cost to break down the wall, and so forth. As bricks are eliminated, the client may have the desire and courage to add additional goals to his or her list.

Goals
Complete education
Marry
Run a marathon
Job promotion
Children
Financial security
Friendship

FIGURE 9.1. Begin with a stick figure and a list of goals.

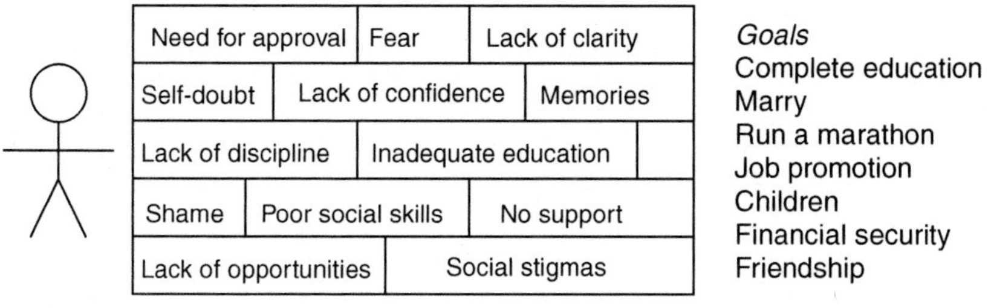

Need for approval	Fear	Lack of clarity	
Self-doubt	Lack of confidence	Memories	
Lack of discipline	Inadequate education		
Shame	Poor social skills	No support	
Lack of opportunities	Social stigmas		

Goals
Complete education
Marry
Run a marathon
Job promotion
Children
Financial security
Friendship

FIGURE 9.2. Add the brick wall barrier.

VIGNETTE

Jake came to therapy expressing general discouragement with his life. He was now thirty-two years old and still hadn't accomplished his dream of finishing college and finding a high-paying job in the computer industry. In fact, he was working as a sales clerk in a mall department store and barely making ends meet. He had a girlfriend and had considered proposing marriage but felt he wasn't financially stable enough to make such a move. In his early twenties, Jake had actually started college twice, each time dropping out after one semester. He had finally given up, wondering if he were really smart enough to compete academically.

Jake was renting a studio apartment and knew that his upwardly mobile girlfriend wouldn't be satisfied with that. He wasn't even satisfied with that himself. Jake was beginning to feel depressed and it was getting more and more difficult to go to work and socialize with his friends. He knew he needed help, but when he came to therapy, he was very apologetic about being there. He wasn't able to clearly state why he wanted help, other than he felt his life was going nowhere.

THERAPIST: Jake, I'm noticing your head bowed and your eyes avoiding me. Can you share with me what you're feeling about being here?

JAKE: Well, I feel like you must think I'm wasting your time. I can't even tell you exactly why I'm here, other than I'm not getting ahead in my life and I'm feeling discouraged.

THERAPIST: That's a perfectly good enough reason to be in therapy. You also mentioned that you've been feeling depressed lately. When did those symptoms start?

JAKE: When my girlfriend began pressuring me to propose. I know she wants a nice home, children, the works, and I know that I can't provide those things, at least not now. And I began thinking that if she's not happy with me the way I am now, maybe the relationship just isn't meant to be. Except I have to admit, I'm not happy with myself.

THERAPIST: Jake, let's get a little background history.

Jake complied and told the therapist that his early school years were dismal due to a learning disability that made it difficult to comprehend anything he read. Although he had managed to graduate from high school with Cs, it had been a huge struggle. Jake felt that his parents were ashamed of him because his older brother always made straight As with ease. Jake was teased a lot due to being in special education classes and admitted that in high school, he began smoking marijuana and drinking beer to try to fit in with his peers. He hadn't dated much until a few years ago and, at thirty-two, was feeling a lot of pressure from his family as well as his girlfriend to marry and "settle down."

THERAPIST: Jake, let's use an illustration to try to get a handle on what's going on with you.

JAKE: Sure. Visual aids have always made things easier for me to understand.

THERAPIST: You've mentioned that you are discouraged with where you are in your life. Can you tell me what your goals are?

JAKE: Well, I'll try. But they seem unrealistic at this point.

THERAPIST: Never mind about that. We'll look at the reality of your goals later.

Jake and the therapist created the illustration shown in Figure 9.3.

Jake began to warm up as he described goals he'd dreamed about years ago. However, almost immediately, he began to discount his ability to accomplish any of them.

THERAPIST: Jake, it sounds like you're very aware that something's keeping you away from your goals, even though you can't specifically identify whatever it is.

JAKE: You're right. It feels like there's a huge wall between me and my goals and I can't climb over it.

THERAPIST: Jake, you're ahead of me. There is a wall between you and your goals. But let's think of it as being made of bricks, with each brick a barrier that's defeating you at the moment.

Jake listed the barriers to his success (see Figure 9.4).

Goals
Finish college
Own a house
Have a retirement plan
Maybe have children
Get married
Satisfying job
Black belt in martial arts
Travel to China

FIGURE 9.3. Jake's goals.

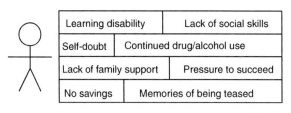

Goals
Finish college
Own a house
Have a retirement plan
Maybe have children
Get married
Satisfying job
Black belt in martial arts
Travel to China

FIGURE 9.4. Jake's brick wall.

JAKE: That's quite a brick wall! How can I ever get over that? I almost feel like giving up.

THERAPIST: I understand your reaction, Jake. But this should be quite encouraging. We've put a name to all the bricks, which means they're real. When the bricks have no names, there's nothing to work with. Now we can look at each brick, one at a time, and work to remove it. Once the wall's down, there should be nothing keeping you from reaching your goals.

JAKE: I see what you mean. When I came in here, I just knew nothing was happening for me but didn't really know why. This at least lets me know what I'm up against.

Diagnosis: Depressive disorder NOS (not otherwise specified)
                Substance abuse
                Reading disorder
Goals: Relief from depressive symptoms
                Abstinence from substances

Ability to read at a high-school level
Improved decision-making skills
Interventions: Alcohol and drug treatment on an outpatient basis
Attendance at Alcoholics Anonymous (AA)/
Narcotics Anonymous (NA) meetings
Meet with a specialized reading tutor once per
week to improve reading skills
Cognitive-behavioral therapy to address depres-
sive symptoms
Problem-solving skills training
Self-esteem work

Initially, Jake didn't see the connection between his marijuana and alcohol use and his lack of motivation. However, he trusted the judgment of his therapist and agreed to engage in outpatient treatment. Once he became clean and sober, he realized how much clearer his thinking was. The drug/alcohol treatment plus the cognitive-behavioral therapy he engaged in with his therapist significantly helped his depressive symptoms; it was decided that antidepressants would not be necessary. It took some time before Jake began to experience improved self-confidence, but when he did, his life began to change significantly. He broke off his relationship with his girlfriend, telling her he needed to work on his own personal growth before he could commit to a serious relationship. Although this was very difficult for Jake, he appreciated the freedom to begin dismantling his brick wall of barriers.

SUGGESTIONS FOR FOLLOW-UP

Jake had many obstacles to overcome and he needed significant follow-up work to provide him with the support he required to completely dismantle his brick wall of barriers. Eventually, Jake invited his parents and brother to therapy for a family session. He was able to share his struggles with them and finally began to receive the support from them which he had longed for all his life. They had never really understood why Jake never seemed to accomplish anything. He also continued to seek support from his AA/NA groups to remain clean and sober. His drug/alcohol treatment program had helped him see that he had been in denial about the extent of his substance abuse problems.

Some of Jake's goals had involved having a family of his own. This frightened him, as he didn't feel equipped to have a healthy relationship with a woman. When Jake did meet an exceptional woman, he returned to therapy for help with getting the relationship off to a positive beginning. His future wife appreciated this about him and he benefited greatly from the respect and admiration she gave him. Jake did have to modify some of his goals. Even with the help of a special reading tutor, he was never able to master the reading skills he needed for a computer degree. Instead, he learned to accept his disability in a realistic manner and began exploring other types of careers that were more suitable to his skills.

CONTRAINDICATIONS FOR USE

Jake almost became overwhelmed when he saw the extent of his problems written on his Brick Wall of Barriers. It is important to discern how much the client can handle. If his or her ego strength seems minimal, begin with only a few of the bricks being named. One can always add to the wall as the client gains the internal strength to handle the problems. If a client is in a major depression, he or she may not have the motivation or ability to look into the future and establish goals. This, in itself, may be overly discouraging. In order for the Brick Wall of Barriers to be an effective illustration, the future must be enticing and something to look forward to. Finally, one needs tools to tear down brick walls. The therapist will need to equip the client with the necessary tools if the client doesn't come prepared. Trying to tear down a brick wall with one's bare hands can cause serious injury. Therefore, the therapist will need to be the construction foreman guiding the client in the demolition process.

Chapter 10

Bloom Where You're Planted

OBJECTIVE

At times, many of us find ourselves in circumstances that are seemingly less than optimal for reaching our goals or achieving life satisfaction. The Bloom Where You're Planted illustration demonstrates how to accurately assess those circumstances and how to thrive in spite of them.

RATIONALE

It is human nature to want our lives to be fairly easy, comfortable, and rewarding at all times. However, most of us would admit that this is an unrealistic expectation. A small minority may come close to this ideal on occasion, but the majority of people go through times in their lives when the "easy life" is so far removed, it isn't even a fantasy. Hopefully, these times will be short-lived. But when they occur, it can be very helpful to gain an objective evaluation of the situation and help to bring forth the most positive outcome possible. The Bloom Where You're Planted illustration can be an invaluable aid in that process.

Not only is dealing with stressful life situations a challenge, but so is promoting personal growth in spite of "life." Is there a way to come through pestilence or storms and still sprout a healthy, strong stalk from deep, tenacious roots? The answer is absolutely. In fact, without challenges, there's little reason or motivation to build strong roots that will eventually grow into a beautiful plant.

On the surface it may seem quite easy to evaluate our strengths and weaknesses, assets and obstacles. Then we just determine where to

Published by The Haworth Press, Inc., 2006. All rights reserved.
doi:10.1300/5397_10

go from there, right? No! Especially under stress, our blind side frequently kicks in and makes it almost impossible to accurately assess our situation alone. It is also difficult to see what future obstacles might be awaiting us. For this example, crows might be an obstacle, or clouds may hide the sun temporarily. Both inhibit growth. The Bloom Where You're Planted illustration graphically depicts what assets we have to work with, what it will take to nurture these assets, and what obstacles might sabotage our efforts. We might be starting either as a seed or a hothouse plant, but both can blossom with gorgeous colors in their seasons.

People familiar with agricultural principles will recognize that different plants require different types of soils and nutrients to produce optimal growth. People are born with different personalities, different talents, and different genetic makeups. These characteristics will play out differently depending on the soil in which they're planted. For example, hydrangeas will produce either a purple blossom or a pink blossom depending on the acidity of the soil, but the basic plant is the same in both cases. Nutrients that we require as human beings start with the basics, such as milk, clean diapers, love, and security. Depending on the type of plants we are, we will require additional nutrients as we age. Someone born with musical talent will require music lessons and training to bloom as a Mozart later in life.

In an ideal world, we have parents who act as our gardeners, watering us and providing the appropriate nutrients for our growth. Gardeners pull weeds that would steal our nutrients for themselves and try to take over our environment. They also protect us from pestilence and hailstorms that would threaten our survival. As we grow, outside forces in addition to the gardeners determine the strength of our stalks and the hardiness of our leaves and blossoms. The sun and gentle rains might represent close, supportive friendships. Bees that help with pollination might represent teachers and other influential adults in our lives. Of course, crows and other birds might steal the seeds and fruits we produce to feed themselves and their own families, with total disrespect of the work it took the plant to get that far. Droughts, blizzards, hail, and extreme temperatures threaten our survival. Our gardeners may leave us to go to other gardens.

In spite of these threats to existence and growth, plants can be very resilient for quite some time. They will grow toward the sun and will send roots deeper to find water if necessary. They might develop natural defenses to keep predators away, such as odors or thorns. Sometimes, finding our way to personal growth through stressful situations requires taking a unique look at situations, differently from how we've seen them before. That's where the Bloom Where You're Planted illustration comes in. It provides a different picture, a different angle or perspective from which to take stock of the scene.

BLOOM WHERE YOU'RE PLANTED
EXERCISE INSTRUCTIONS

All seeds and plants need a pot of nutritious soil to start with, and the Bloom Where You're Planted illustration is no exception (see Figure 10.1). At this point, discuss with the client the known elements needed for growth. Examples are rain, sunlight, pollination, and plant food (see Figure 10.2).

Finally, what are the threats to the plant's growth? Weeds that steal the nutrients for themselves, birds that snatch away the seeds before they can take root, and the absence of rain and sunshine are obvious ones (see Figure 10.3). Have the client identify any threats in his or her own life that might hinder growth. These can be either genuine threats or perceived ones.

VIGNETTE

Alison had been diagnosed with breast cancer three months prior to beginning therapy. Since that horrible day when she first received the diagnosis, her life had resembled a hurricane. A biopsy had revealed the further bad news that the cancer had spread to at least one of her lymph nodes; a radical mastectomy was the result. Alison was

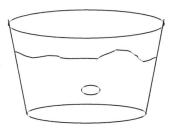

FIGURE 10.1. A seed planted in nutritious soil.

FIGURE 10.2. Elements needed for growth.

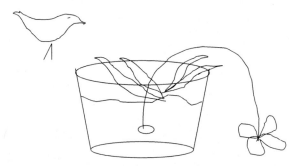

FIGURE 10.3. Threats to plant growth and health.

now undergoing chemotherapy and had become quite depressed. She came to therapy feeling that her life was over. Essentially, Alison's goals for therapy were to help prepare her family for her death and help herself come to a place of spiritual peace while she still had time.

Alison's therapist got her permission to consult with her oncologist to discuss a course of treatment. The oncologist was very surprised to hear of Alison's emotional and psychological condition. Although he knew she was depressed, he had no idea of her preparations for death. In fact, the oncologist had just shared with Alison a couple of weeks ago that in addition to the successful surgery, her chemotherapy was also having beneficial effects. He had gladly shared the prognosis with Alison that she had many good years ahead of her. Apparently, Alison had not yet absorbed the positive implications of that meeting. The oncologist was quite willing to work with the therapist to treat Alison's depression and prescribed an antidepressant.

When the therapist shared with Alison the consultation with the oncologist, Alison quickly dismissed her doctor's input. "Believe it or not, the doctor has a hard time dealing with death. I'm sure he tells all his patients they're going to get better. But I can feel the truth of the matter inside me and don't need his false reassurance," Alison stated. The therapist recognized a thick wall of defenses when she saw one and knew that it would be difficult work ahead for her and Alison. She didn't challenge Alison's beliefs initially, but figured she had her defenses in place for a reason. Of course, the truth was that Alison herself was terrified of dying.

ALISON: I'm only forty-four years old. I'm not ready to die and I'm not ready to change my life from the way it used to be. I loved my life. I have a wonderful family. I was a teacher and loved my job. I have a beautiful home. All of that is gone and I admit I can't handle it.

THERAPIST: Is it true that everything has changed? Don't you still have a wonderful family and a beautiful home? Aren't you still a teacher? Maybe things are just different and not gone.

ALISON: Well, I can't take care of my home and it may have to be sold to pay medical bills. I'm not ready to go back to work yet, I can't bear everyone feeling sorry for me. And my family's tired of all this. I wouldn't blame them if they left.

THERAPIST: Alison, it sounds like the loss of the familiar and loved is overwhelming right now. Grief is a normal part of an experience with cancer. Let's work through that together.

The therapist convinced Alison to join a cancer support group that focused on working through the grief. They also worked on it in individual therapy, particularly the depression. She was compliant with her antidepressant medication and within a month, began to feel better. Alison was willing to include her family in therapy and the therapist worked with them to help support Alison in the new life changes she was having to face.

THERAPIST: Alison, it has been a long, tough road to get to a place where you can accept the changes in your life. I'm delighted to see you feeling better and now, it's time to think of moving forward.

ALISON: What do you mean, "moving forward"? I'm finally able to get up in the morning and leave the house without crying. I'm no longer frightened of losing my family or my home. I don't know how much more forward I can go.

THERAPIST: Alison, you have now accepted the fact that you had cancer, major surgery, and chemotherapy. And you survived. But life is more than surviving! Things are different for you and this experience has changed the way you think about life and death forever. I want to encourage you to consider embracing your life this side of cancer and learn to love it as much as you loved your life before.

ALISON: That sounds impossible, but I'm listening.

THERAPIST: I would like to demonstrate what I'm talking about with an illustration. Imagine you're a seed, beginning your life again. You're in a rich pot of soil and ready to sprout.

ALISON: I'm with you. I enjoy gardening and always wanted to smell like a gardenia.

THERAPIST: Well, now's your chance. Let's talk about what nutrients and conditions you will need in order to grow into a strong, healthy plant.

Together Alison and her therapist looked at all of her strengths and the resources that were available to her. She had learned that her family was in this with her for the long haul and had finally accepted that their love was unconditional. She had reestablished her spiritual faith through her ordeal and had a sense of peace which had been missing for a long time. Alison had accepted that she might need to continue her antidepressant medication for a time and appreciated the support of her medical team. After this, Alison began laughing and said, "I feel like doing a commercial for Miracle-Gro! I'm feeling ashamed of myself. I've had many of these things available to me for years and never recognized it."

THERAPIST: That brings us to the next part of this illustration. We now have to look at the predators and obstacles that might stunt your growth. Unwarranted shame is one of those obstacles. It is nothing to be ashamed about when we gain new eyes for the blessings within us and around us. Birds are predators that can snatch the seeds and new plant shoots before they can take firm root and develop into strong stalks. One example of a predator might be a person who constantly raises doubt about your prognosis, who consistently criticizes your treatment plan and treats you as more ill than you are.

ALISON: Edith. She's an elderly neighbor whose husband died ten years ago of lung cancer. I've learned I can't visit with her anymore. She's so bitter about her husband's death that she's given up on anything joyous in life. She has always seemed angry that I had successful treatment and got better. I was feeling guilty about sharing any good news with her and also guilty if I avoided visiting her.

THERAPIST: Great example. Another threat to growth is drought. Don't be afraid to enjoy new things in your life within any physical limitations you might have. Getting stuck in the same old routines can stunt your growth. On the other hand, don't overdo it. Too much rain can produce rot. It's all about balance, the right kind and amount of nutrients along with the right kind and amount of external encouragements.

Diagnosis:	Major depression associated with a medical condition
	Bereavement
Goals:	Resolution of depressive symptoms
	Grief management
	Healthy adjustment to surviving cancer
Interventions:	Cognitive-behavioral therapy to treat depressive symptoms
	Grief therapy, including participation in a cancer/grief support group
	Family therapy to help Alison with major life changes
	Individual therapy to address personal-growth issues

Alison and her therapist continued their work with the Bloom Where You're Planted illustration. The creative nature of the illustration stimulated Alison's imagination to see the possibilities of her life after cancer. She also clearly understood the need to nurture and care for her new growth. The vivid image of becoming a fragrant gardenia became fixed in Alison's mind and provided her with the motivation to try new and innovative activities. She loved teaching but felt that going back to her third-grade classroom was more stress than she wanted to deal with. So she diverted her skills into working part-time for the American Cancer Society, leading educational support groups. She also taught religious classes at her church. She and her family became more creative in how they spent their leisure time together, appreciating one another in wonderful new ways. Alison discovered that joy exists in the growing of the flower, not only in the final product.

SUGGESTIONS FOR FOLLOW-UP

Alison relapsed after three years. Another cancerous lesion was discovered in her right lung and required additional chemotherapy. Although Alison experienced discouragement and mild depressive symptoms again, they did not return to the severity of her previous illness. Alison returned to therapy for support and encouragement. The Bloom Where You're Planted illustration reminded her to be creative in her perspective on life. It had taught her to be alert to any dangers that might threaten her growth. The illustration was also a clear guide to helping her think through what would help her build strength within.

As new storm clouds hovered over Alison's gardenia, threatening to drown her in a downpour, she came up with the idea of erecting an umbrella over her plant. This was a time in her life when she recognized the need for extra protection and also knew that strength could be found in asking for help. Alison asked her family, her medical team, her therapist, her friends, and her pastor to be that umbrella for her. She shared the Bloom Where You're Planted illustration with each of them so they could understand her perspective of growth.

CONTRAINDICATIONS FOR USE

As you can see from this case, a person must be ready to look toward the future before engaging in this illustration. The Bloom Where You're Planted illustration is all about strong growth based from the pot you're planted in. Those clients suffering from severe depression, grief, and psychosis may not benefit from this illustration until these conditions have been adequately treated. When ready to begin using the illustration, the therapist will also need to ensure that clients are well connected with reality in their lives. Sometimes with such a graphic illustration as this one, clients can find it too easy to escape into fantasy and negate the purpose of the illustration.

Chapter 11

The Pressure Box

OBJECTIVE

Although it is possible that people from any era of time would argue that theirs was the most stressful time in which to live, the twenty-first century is likely to head that list from almost any perspective. The Pressure Box illustration gives one the feeling of what it is like to have the walls of stress closing in from every direction. The illustration can then be used as a base to determine what strengths are required to keep the walls of stress at bay or even a comfortable distance away.

RATIONALE

The notion of stress has been a topic in the forefront of both physical medicine and mental health practice for many years. Research in the twentieth century has confirmed the damage that stress can cause both physically and emotionally. Ulcers, headaches, and panic attacks often have their roots in stress. Stress management is a hot topic for seminars in the corporate world. In times past, people certainly endured the stress of drought, flooding, lack of jobs, crops failing, women dying during childbirth, wild animal attacks, and so forth. Handling those events stoically was considered a virtue, but not anymore. We now encourage people to talk about their stress, to learn to manage it, and to treat it with medication if necessary.

In spite of the openness with which our culture now deals with stress, many of us are still reluctant to admit their situations. This may partially be due to pride in wanting to keep our vulnerabilities private or a lack of knowledge about resources that can help. It may also be

Published by The Haworth Press, Inc., 2006. All rights reserved.
doi:10.1300/5397_11

that the stress itself is so overwhelming that people hardly have the strength to drag themselves to therapy or a doctor's office. The Pressure Box illustration demonstrates what it might feel like to be "boxed in" by stressful situations. The space often feels confining and it may seem to have no doors or windows from which to escape. While inside this confining box, people may hear and feel the pressure from stressors pushing the walls in ever closer around them. What a frightening experience that can be! It is all too easy to feel defeated in such a situation.

A popular movie from several years ago had a scene in which three space-age heroes found themselves falling into a large garbage receptacle in their attempts to get away from the enemy soldiers. Upon discovering their situation, the enemy soldiers flipped a switch to cause the receptacle walls to begin closing in, ostensibly to compact the "trash." The heroes were scrambling to find anything they could to keep the walls at bay. Of course, they found a way of escape. They had a sequel to prepare for. It is more rare than not that a way of escape cannot be found in stressful situations. However, the nature of stress is that it blinds us to alternatives that might save our lives.

In the Pressure Box illustration, the therapist first helps the client to identify the causes, or "arrows" of stress. It is difficult to fight an enemy that has no name. Helping the client slow down enough to label the stress, locate its source, describe it, and discuss its possible consequences is the beginning of finding a solution or escape. Stress generates tremendous amounts of fear and anxiety, which stifle productivity in problem solving. Fear and anxiety can easily lead to cognitive distortions, which make it even more difficult to escape the box. Having an objective person (the therapist) outside the box and coaching the client to think clearly, can be very helpful. The client can strengthen his or her arms to keep the walls at bay, can find a tool to keep the walls from further compressing, and can learn the skills to build a door for escape.

In using the Pressure Box illustration in therapy, the therapist assists the client to deal with every arrow of stress that is threatening his or her survival. In the drawing, as each arrow falls away from the box, the client can visually experience the relief from the stress. A certain amount of stress is normal for optimal functioning. It challenges us to continually use our minds in the creative activities of problem solving and personal growth. Without a few arrows applying pressure to hold the walls up, they might collapse upon us, leading to a deadly outcome. The therapist will need to work with the client to determine which arrows are healthy supports and which ones need to be knocked away. Some of the arrows will need to remain in place but have their shafts shortened to decrease the pressure. Ideally, the final outcome in this scenario is the client becoming the proactive builder of the box, making the decisions about which materials to use for the box and which ones to discard.

THE PRESSURE BOX
EXERCISE INSTRUCTIONS

Although the Pressure Box illustration itself is a simple drawing, it has many angles on which a therapist can focus. In the beginning, draw a basic box with a stick figure inside. Also draw a few arrows that represent normal stressors, as in Figure 11.1.

Explain to the client that we all need a structure that provides a certain amount of pressure to our lives. The pressure of the atmosphere keeps our feet on the ground rather than floating in space. The pressure caused by hunger motivates us to work to find food. The pressure of feeling cold motivates us to build a fire and put on warm clothes. This is all normal and necessary. However, sometimes, additional pressures begin to shoot at us. At this point, draw the arrows directed at the box. Then work with the client to help him or her name the arrows with the stressors they're experiencing.

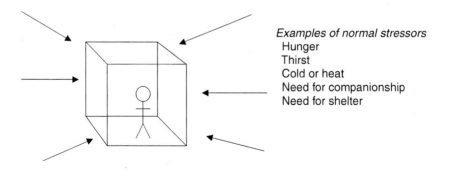

Examples of normal stressors
Hunger
Thirst
Cold or heat
Need for companionship
Need for shelter

FIGURE 11.1. The Pressure Box illustration.

The therapist will need to help the client examine each stressor in depth to help him or her determine whether it is a healthy stressor or whether it is a stressor draining him or her of resources, energy, and peace of mind (see Figure 11.2). Stress-management techniques unique to the client's situation can be developed by working as a team. As each stressor is dealt with, draw that arrow falling away from the Pressure Box (see Figure 11.3). Remind the client that a few normal stressors need to remain in place in order to keep the box from collapsing and to maintain its shape.

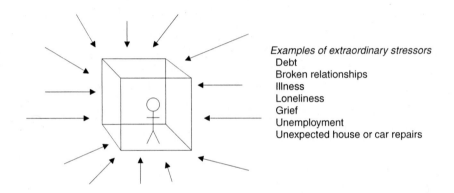

Examples of extraordinary stressors
Debt
Broken relationships
Illness
Loneliness
Grief
Unemployment
Unexpected house or car repairs

FIGURE 11.2. Stressors that are unhealthy can take a great toll.

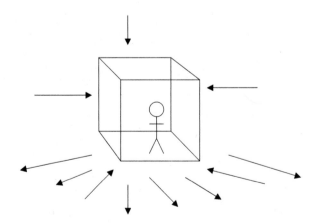

FIGURE 11.3. Some stressors can be alleviated, which reduces the pressure in the box.

VIGNETTE

Bruce was a twenty-three-year-old graduate student at a prestigious university. He came to therapy complaining of stress and anxiety with symptoms of insomnia, hand tremors, sweating, and loss of appetite with occasional vomiting and diarrhea. Bruce had only two semesters left to complete his degree but was considering dropping out of school if his situation didn't improve. The thought of disappointing his parents, who were working-class people that had sacrificed considerably for him to go to school, was unbearable. He also had a serious girlfriend who was pressuring him to make a permanent commitment to her and he knew that without completing his education, it would be difficult to get a good-paying job to support them.

Bruce was clearly desperate as he laid this scenario before the therapist. He admitted to worrying about more things than he could list in the time allotted. Even though his parents were doing what they could to help, Bruce was up to his neck in school loans. His degree would be a somewhat specialized area of art history. He could earn a good salary with many benefits as a museum director, but his course work was of little practical use without the degree. He was behind in his assignments and had missed several days at his part-time job because of his stomach upsets. On top of all this, Bruce had just been told by his girlfriend that she thought she was pregnant.

THERAPIST: You seem to be in considerable distress, Bruce. Can you please be a little more specific about when the symptoms began and any precipitating factors that might have triggered them?

BRUCE: I'll try. I think this started when I began dating Jennifer six months ago. The relationship just got too intense too fast. I'd never dated much and I think I was so lonely and flattered that she was interested in me, I just began letting my responsibilities go in order to be with her. Then I began to feel guilty that I was letting my grades slip and not going home as frequently as I was to visit my parents.

THERAPIST: That's understandable. It sounds like you're very close to your parents. Do they like Jennifer?

BRUCE: I guess I'm close to them. They're very possessive. They took out a second mortgage on their house to finance my graduate school education and their expectations of me are very high. I've been lying to them about my grades falling. To be honest, I haven't even told them about Jennifer. I know they don't want me to be distracted with dating until I finish school. Jennifer's upset with me, accusing me of being ashamed to introduce her to my family. That's really not it at all. Now she's telling me she might be pregnant. I'm telling you, I feel I'm in a constant state of panic most of the time now.

THERAPIST: Your story sounds quite complicated. What if we use a drawing to help us sort things out?

BRUCE: I do love art. Let's go with it.

THERAPIST: Well, this isn't Picasso, but hopefully it will visually clarify the problem and then help us find a solution.

The therapist drew the Pressure Box and explained the notion of normal stress as a motivator to success. Bruce understood the concept and had indeed made good use of it until recently. Then she added the additional stressor arrows. Although he laughed good-naturedly at the simplicity of the drawing, he got the message and began naming the arrows. He began to panic as the drawing impacted him, and the therapist had to help him with some deep-breathing exercises before continuing (see Figure 11.4).

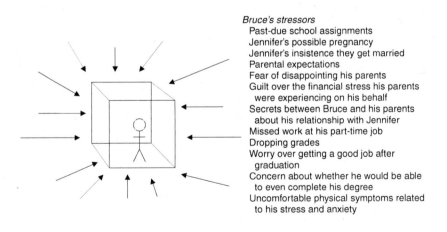

Bruce's stressors
Past-due school assignments
Jennifer's possible pregnancy
Jennifer's insistence they get married
Parental expectations
Fear of disappointing his parents
Guilt over the financial stress his parents
  were experiencing on his behalf
Secrets between Bruce and his parents
  about his relationship with Jennifer
Missed work at his part-time job
Dropping grades
Worry over getting a good job after
  graduation
Concern about whether he would be able
  to even complete his degree
Uncomfortable physical symptoms related
  to his stress and anxiety

FIGURE 11.4. Bruce's Pressure Box.

BRUCE: I can't believe this! No wonder I've been panicking. What can I do other than just give up and run away?

THERAPIST: Although this appears overwhelming, we now actually have something concrete with which to work. Let's take each of these stressors one at a time, examining all aspects of what they mean in your life, and then determine what actions might be helpful.

This took a considerable amount of time for Bruce to complete. He came to recognize that even though he was twenty-three years old, he had still not separated from his parents emotionally in order to begin his adult life. As their only child, they had resisted helping him with this process. Bruce also discovered that although he was quite intelligent, he had not been using his intellect to develop solid organizational skills. This was costing him precious time in getting his assignments completed and negotiating his work schedule. Bruce also recognized that inadequate social skills had led to him making some poor choices in his relationship with Jennifer. He admitted that he needed to set some firmer boundaries with her, which would lead to a more mutually respectful relationship.

BRUCE: Do you think it's too late for me to knock some of those arrows away before they cave in my walls?

THERAPIST: Not at all. You may have some difficult choices to make and even some unpleasant consequences resulting from previous choices, but it's definitely not too late to turn things around.

Diagnosis:	Anxiety disorder, NOS
	Partner relational problem
Goals:	Resolution of anxiety symptoms
	Successful completion of his education
	Begin the separation-individuation process with his parents
	Appropriate stress management
	Development of a healthy relationship with Jennifer
Interventions:	Individual therapy to process relationship with his parents

Family therapy to promote a more adult relation-
ship with both his parents and Jennifer
Educational counseling
Stress-management training
Social-skills training
Consultation with Bruce's physician to evaluate
the potential need for medication management

Bruce experienced immediate relief when he discovered that Jennifer's potential pregnancy was a false alarm. They wanted to continue seeing each other but both recognized that the relationship
needed firmer boundaries and some distance while they each worked
on personal issues. Meetings with Bruce's parents were difficult and
their relationship became strained for a time. Eventually, they began
to rebuild the connection slowly. Bruce arranged a meeting with his
graduate school adviser and they worked out a plan for him to complete his makeup work. He took a leave of absence from his job until
his symptoms improved. In addition, Bruce did take some antianxiety
medication and found it helpful as he tackled these difficult problems.
However, he found he didn't need the medication for long, as he worked
hard to learn better stress-management techniques in therapy.

SUGGESTIONS FOR FOLLOW-UP

Once the immediate problems were under control and Bruce felt
more solid in his new stress-management techniques, his therapist
suggested they go back to the Pressure Box drawing and reanalyze
it. The therapist helped Bruce examine the materials used to build
the Pressure Box in the first place. Indeed, they seemed flimsy and
did not meet accepted building codes. As an only child, Bruce had
been indulged and had not learned some of the basic life skills he
needed as a foundation to build relationships and negotiate problems. He had never considered what his own value system was apart
from his parents.

Bruce found it very productive to dismantle the Pressure Box and
research what materials he might use to rebuild it in order to with-
stand the pressures and stresses of life. This certainly went beyond
the treatment of his presenting problems, but Bruce saw it as preven-
tative. He humorously likened this process to the story of the three

little pigs, deciding that he wanted his Pressure Box to be built of bricks. "I've totally had enough of the 'Big Bad Wolf' trying to blow my house down!" Bruce declared.

CONTRAINDICATIONS FOR USE

The Pressure Box illustration can be overwhelming for someone of a fragile nature. Clients who have been bombarded with extraordinary stressors might need "shoring up" before being presented with this illustration. The "shoring up" might include medication management and instruction in learning relaxation exercises in order to cope with the impact of the Pressure Box illustration. Patients prone to hysteria and those in deep depressive states may find this illustration too overpowering. It is therefore not recommended for initial treatment of these types of clients.

Chapter 12

Fisherman's Wharf

OBJECTIVE

Some people seem to get easily taken advantage of or are victimized by others for various reasons. The Fisherman's Wharf illustration helps these people get in touch with their feelings of victimization, learn to examine the motives of others, and develop a plan to avoid taking the bait.

RATIONALE

Wouldn't it be wonderful if we could all swim free in our own little oceans without fear of predators? Wonderful, but not always possible. Some fish mitigate the possibility of predators attacking by effectively using their God-given defenses—spines, camouflage, foul odors, speed, sharp teeth, and so forth. Even then, they occasionally get caught off guard or are overpowered. People also have defense mechanisms at their disposal, but sometimes neglect to use them, don't develop them, aren't aware of them, or don't believe in their power to work. This seems illogical. Why wouldn't people protect themselves if they could?

Of course, we might neglect to protect ourselves for many reasons. Some people never learn the skills of using their potential defenses effectively. Some people want so badly to live in a world in which people are always nice and thoughtful to one another that they choose to ignore any signs to the contrary. Some people have such low self-esteem they feel unworthy of being protected. Other reasons also ex-

doi:10.1300/5397_12

ist. Once we've been taken advantage of, it becomes easier and easier to stay in a victim role. Like it or not, selfishness and evil are present in our world.

The Fisherman's Wharf illustration helps clients to identify their victim role, to understand the characteristics of the victim role and the predator role, and to see the consequences of remaining in the victim role. Finally, the illustration is used to help the victim swim away from threatening situations, regaining their freedom to choose where they will swim. Fish have a need for food like any other living creature. They are always on the lookout for a tasty morsel of some sort. This can definitely be an enjoyable experience, or it can be their downfall.

Fishermen (or women) have the purpose of using fish for sport and/or to harm them. They study what might attract the fish and then drop the bait into the water. What is important to remember about bait is that it's often fake, imitation, and deceptive. It never really satisfies a fish's desire for tasty, nourishing food, but it certainly mimics the real thing. Even if live bait is used, there's always a hook in there somewhere. Once the fish takes the bait, the fisherman is in total control of the situation. The hook will inevitably injure the fish and unless it is rescued and treated, it will die. Ultimately, the fish will be rendered incapable of doing what fish were created to do—swim.

This is naturally much more complicated for human beings. For one, we have more complex needs than fish. Therefore, the fisherman has more options of bait from which to choose. This translates into more dangers for humans to sort through. Does this mean that we always have to be on guard, never able to safely enjoy a good swim without looking over our fins? No, but it does mean we need to choose our oceans carefully. We also need to work on developing good swimming techniques. The only way for a fish to escape being caught by the bait is to recognize it for what it is and swim away. For humans, swimming techniques might include good social and communication skills, knowing how to maintain appropriate boundaries with others, knowing how to confront would-be predators effectively, and knowing when to ask for help from others. A school of fish is definitely more difficult to fool than a solitary swimmer.

FISHERMAN'S WHARF
EXERCISE INSTRUCTIONS

As with the other drawings in this book, the Fisherman's Wharf illustration is simple to draw, although the visual effect can be very powerful. First of all, draw the ocean with a fish in it (see Figure 12.1). Begin to explore with the client the characteristics of a fish. For example, fish were made for swimming. The therapist might ask the client about his or her natural talents and desires for the future.

Next, draw the wharf with the fisherman (or woman) (as in Figure 12.2). Explore with the client the characteristics of a fisherman. For example, the fisherman has the agenda to catch a fish and may spend considerable time learning the likes and dislikes of the fish in question in order to choose the most attractive bait.

Now, draw the fisherman with his or her fishing pole and the hook on the end (see Figure 12.3). Discuss with the client how the fisherman

FIGURE 12.1. Fisherman's Wharf basic illustration.

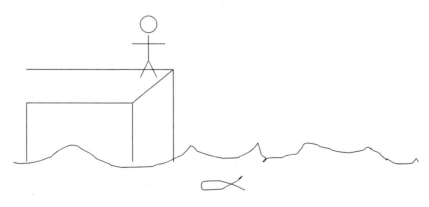

FIGURE 12.2. The fisherman appears.

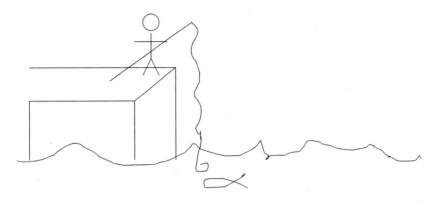

FIGURE 12.3. The fisherman uses bait to lure his prey.

might use his or her knowledge about the fish to choose the most effective equipment and bait to use. For example, some fish might be attracted by colorful, flashy lures. Similarly, a young girl might be convinced to go with a stranger who has an expensive, bright red sports car if he promises to let her drive it. Other bait might target sensitive emotions. A youngster might be convinced to lie for his drug-using parents if they promise him a hug afterward.

At this point, the therapist needs to help the client personalize the illustration. Discuss areas of weakness that might cause the client to be vulnerable to taking the bait. Help the client learn how to recognize bait (imitation) from genuine resources that will meet his or her needs. Finally, work with the client to improve his or her swimming techniques. They can learn new strokes, do exercises to strengthen the strokes they already know, and learn to identify safe oceans in which to swim. This puts the client in the best position to swim safely and enjoyably, being able to effectively utilize his or her gifts and talents in life.

VIGNETTE

Tammy was a thirty-three-year-old single mother of two who came to therapy after being date-raped at a bar two weeks earlier. She still appeared to be in a state of shock and admitted she would never have made the appointment without the strong encouragement of the rape crisis team at the hospital emergency room where she had received treatment. Even then, it took her more than a week to pick up the phone. Tammy's children were six and eight years old and she loved them dearly. She felt very embarrassed and ashamed that she had placed herself in this situation at the bar. In fact, Tammy totally blamed herself for everything that had happened. She had identified the man involved, but had refused to press charges because she felt it was her own fault.

Tammy cried her way through most of the first session, hardly able to share any details of what had happened, although they were obviously burned deeply in her memory. She reluctantly agreed to come back, although she didn't believe at this point that anyone could help her. Tammy's self-esteem and sense of self-worth were so low that the therapist suspected more was behind this than the recent rape, which was bad enough in itself. However, she didn't press the issue at this point. Tammy returned and they began work to help her recover from the date rape. Tammy eventually agreed to attend a support group at the local rape crisis center and found that helpful as well.

After several weeks of treatment, Tammy had returned to her job and felt able to care for her children, but she still was not bouncing back emotionally. She still refused to press charges against the rapist, and flashbacks continued to prevent her from getting adequate rest. The therapist gently asked Tammy if other things from her past might be bothering her in addition to her recent trauma. Again, Tammy broke down in tears and admitted that many things from her past were troubling her. She had built enough trust in the therapist by this time that she was willing to explore these other painful areas. The therapist began taking a more detailed history of Tammy's life and discovered she had indeed opened a Pandora's box of painful memories.

Tammy's mother was an alcoholic and had left Tammy's father to pursue multiple boyfriends over the years. Her father had not wanted full custody of Tammy but only occasional visits. Unfortunately, beginning when Tammy was five years old, she was taken advantage of sexually by two or three of her mother's boyfriends while her mother typically lay on the couch in a drunken stupor. This went on for four years until eventually her mother was reported to the Department of Social Services and Tammy was placed in a foster home. She had stayed in several foster homes by the time she graduated from high school (at the bottom of her class). Tammy totally blamed herself for her history, believing that these events never would have happened if she had been a more likeable child.

THERAPIST: Tammy, thank you for sharing this history. It was obviously a very difficult thing for you to do. It certainly clarifies why this recent traumatic event in your life had such powerful negative effects on you. But it also provides us with valuable information that I believe we can use to help you.

TAMMY: I feel like such damaged goods that nothing can help. The only reason I've wanted to stay alive is knowing that my own children need me to protect them and care for them.

THERAPIST: Well, Tammy, that's good motivation to begin seeing if you can be helped. I believe it's more than possible, but I'll be honest, it will be hard work.

TAMMY: I guess for my kids' sake, I'm willing to give it a try. Where do we start?

THERAPIST: It sounds like you have been a victim of abuse on and off throughout your life. One of the most important parts of recovery is leaving that victim role behind. Let's use a drawing to help you visualize what I mean.

Tammy agreed and the therapist drew the Fisherman's Wharf illustration. Her shame made it difficult to maintain eye contact with the therapist, but being able to focus on the drawing gave Tammy some emotional distance from the dreadful personal information she had shared. Tammy shyly admitted that her one main talent in life was singing. She often went to bars on karaoke nights as a way to perform, not having had the confidence to pursue a career in music. When Tammy and her therapist began talking about the motives of the fishermen, she took it from there.

TAMMY: I don't have to be told their motives. It seems like every man I've ever been around has only wanted to use me sexually. Or they sent me on errands to get them drugs and alcohol. My ex-husband only wanted my paycheck so he could lie around on the couch, watching TV and drinking.

THERAPIST: Okay. It sounds like you've had lots of experience with the negative agendas of men. Let's talk about what it was that made you vulnerable to those negative agendas.

TAMMY: I can't remember ever feeling like I was worth doing anything else. I kept hoping that if I got them what they wanted, I might at least get some affection back. It just never happened.

THERAPIST: What a great insight! The negative beliefs you held about yourself made you a logical target for a fisherman. And your very appropriate need for affection led you to take the bait. Once you took the bait, the control was out of your hands.

TAMMY: That makes total sense, but how can I keep from taking the bait? It always looks so appealing at the time.

THERAPIST: Great question, Tammy. First of all, you will need to learn to tell the difference between bait and genuine offers of affection. Then, you will need to learn how to strengthen your swimming skills.

Tammy and her therapist worked for some time on these areas. Tammy slowly began to gain some confidence and belief that she could indeed learn to swim better and avoid taking the bait. She recognized that the only way to avoid further harm to herself was to learn to swim away from the bait. This was quite difficult for Tammy, as her main social connections were fishermen. She eventually admitted that she needed to find a different ocean in which to swim.

Diagnosis: Post-traumatic stress disorder
Goals: Recovery from date-rape trauma
Explore past sexual abuse trauma for the purpose of healing
Develop her latent singing talent
Become a more effective mother
Development of healthy social relationships
Interventions: Crisis work initially to manage symptoms from the date rape
Individual therapy to explore past sexual-abuse trauma
Parenting training
Social-skills training

Coping-skills development
Group therapy for women with a history of sexual abuse when ready

Tammy remained in therapy for more than a year. She had been significantly damaged by her childhood trauma; rebuilding her core beliefs into ones that directed her to a positive future was extremely difficult for her. Initially, she entered this healing journey out of love for her own children, but eventually, she began to enjoy the personal rewards she experienced herself. She changed jobs and moved to a different neighborhood, recognizing the need to find a different ocean for swimming. Tammy also had a great deal to learn about setting strong boundaries with fishermen (or women).

SUGGESTIONS FOR FOLLOW-UP

Tammy required significant follow-up on her road to recovery. She had never had the solid love and support of a family. She frequently checked in with her therapist for reassurance, particularly when she was learning a new swim stroke. Not only did Tammy need to learn better parenting skills to use with her children, but, in a real sense, she needed to learn to parent herself better. The first step away from intensive individual therapy was participation in a women's support group. Tammy found it very helpful to have contact with other women who had gone through similar life experiences. Then the therapist helped her find positive groups in her community through which she could begin to develop a broader base of support in her efforts to heal and become more self-sufficient. Initially, Tammy was quite frightened to trust her own instincts in meeting new people.

Once Tammy was on a more solid footing, her therapist began to suggest that she might benefit from exploring other talents and interests besides singing. When the need for survival was no longer on the front burner of her life, Tammy had the energy to do more self-exploration in a positive sense. She took self-defense classes both for exercise and to gain confidence in caring for herself. She also enrolled in some community college classes to see if she might like to pursue music in a more formal way. She joined the PTA to become more involved with her children and took the huge risk of joining a Parents Without Partners group.

Before long, she began dating a man she met in the group. This caused many painful memories to resurface and she returned to individual therapy for a brief time to work through these issues. Tammy continued to use the Fisherman's Wharf illustration to help her evaluate situations with new people. She would ask herself what their agenda might be and what her own vulnerabilities might be. Tammy shared with her therapist in one of their last sessions that a new question she was asking was, "What swim strokes can I use to escape the bait?" Tammy had learned to value the strengths she had developed and was enjoying swimming for the first time in her life.

CONTRAINDICATIONS FOR USE

As Tammy's case readily demonstrates, clients who have been freshly victimized may be unable to immediately become involved with the Fisherman's Wharf illustration. They will likely need their total energies to stabilize their situation. Clients who are excessively hopeless may find this illustration depressing, feeling they might as well continue to take the bait because they'll never be able to learn to swim away.

Another group of clients who might find the Fisherman's Wharf illustration too difficult is the group who are fishermen (or -women) themselves. The realization of how they've used others for their own selfish purposes may be too overwhelming. To understand visually how they've caused serious injury to fish who only want to swim may be beyond their coping abilities. On the other hand, clients with antisocial personality disorder might find the illustration amusing and use it to feed their imaginations to devise other kinds of bait.

Chapter 13

Pole Vault for Goals

OBJECTIVE

The Pole Vault for Goals illustration is a simple way of visualizing a goal and planning the steps needed to get there. With each step accomplished, the bar gets raised. The Pole Vault for Goals helps clients plan ahead in a reasonable way to obtain the end results they are hoping for.

RATIONALE

The Pole Vault for Goals illustration fits right in with the Olympic concept of having both short- and long-term goals and planning the training program needed to achieve them. Timing is everything, and making plans to reach goals is no exception. No one who participates in the Olympic Games decides a month prior to the Games that it might be a good idea to begin training. Many of these athletes began in childhood to focus on this goal that wouldn't come to fruition for years. Imagine a future pole-vaulter at six years of age telling his or her parents that he or she would someday vault many feet into the air as if he or she were flying. These parents likely laughed, telling their children they would first have to be able to vault onto their bed!

Many people have an all-or-nothing attitude about reaching goals. They either want fairly instant success or they quit and achieve nothing. Most people realize that it takes work, and even some planning, to reach their goals, but are unrealistic in how they proceed. They don't allow enough time, the steps required to reach their goals get out of order, or they don't enlist needed assistance when their knowledge base is limited. For example, a young person might dream of

Published by The Haworth Press, Inc., 2006. All rights reserved.
doi:10.1300/5397_13

being a doctor when he or she grows up, but his or her only vision is of dramatically doing open-heart surgery in the operating room to save a life. If they're just graduating from high school, they may have ten to twelve years before that vision could possibly become true. Even then, without expert help to choose the proper courses and gain the proper work experience, it won't happen. If this young person tries to get there without help, he or she might face a rejection when the medical school discovers he or she never took chemistry.

The Pole Vault for Goals illustration helps clients see the logic in planning for goals in a stepwise progression. With each step mastered, they can easily visualize gaining strength and confidence to vault over a higher bar next time. Eventually, they will be enjoying the goals they dreamed about in the most efficient manner possible. Otherwise, one might hear such remarks as, "That's too hard, I should have known I couldn't do it" or "Why didn't someone tell me I should have taken such and such a class?" or "That will take way more time than I want to put in." It is sad to watch people experiencing disappointment and discouragement from not reaching their goals simply because they refused to plan ahead and get into training.

POLE VAULT FOR GOALS
EXERCISE INSTRUCTIONS

The most important starting point for any goal is to have a target. Therefore, the first step in the Pole Vault for Goals illustration is to draw a target and help the client clearly delineate their goals (see Figure 13.1). Next, draw the training field with a stick figure and the bar before them. As they look up, the height of the bar might appear overwhelming or as a welcome challenge, but it will clearly be out of their reach to begin with (see Figure 13.2).

Some empathy might be in order as the client peers up at the height of the bar—but not for long. Talk with the client about backing off from the final goal and beginning with smaller goals. In other words, start with a much lower bar (see Figure 13.3).

Next, discuss with the client the equipment he or she will need to vault over that bar. Initially, maybe no equipment at all will be needed, a sign that the beginning bar is too low to be any kind of motivating challenge. Help the client choose the right pole for his or her goal—the right

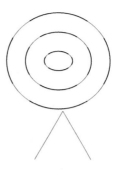

Examples of possible goals
Completing college
Trip to Europe
Marriage and family
Competing in the Olympics

FIGURE 13.1. A target and the client's list of goals.

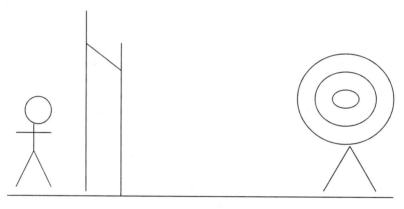

FIGURE 13.2. The bar is too high at first.

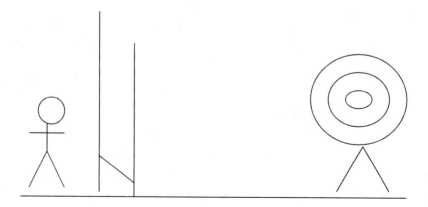

FIGURE 13.3. Start with a smaller, more realistic goal.

weight, height, and width. The equipment will need to be appropriate for his or her talents and physical abilities (see Figure 13.4).

Finally, over time, help the client choose when and how to raise the bar in a logical and realistic manner until the goal is reached. Have the client write on each bar the plan he or she develops to pole-vault over the bar with ease (see Figure 13.5).

VIGNETTE

Ben was going to be a sophomore in high school. His mother had brought him in for therapy due to defiance at home and some cutting

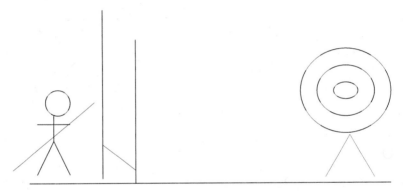

FIGURE 13.4. Choosing the right pole will help with the jump.

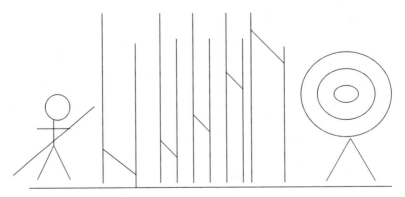

FIGURE 13.5. Each bar represents a goal to strive for.

behavior. She was also worried that he might have started drinking with some friends, of whom she did not approve. Ben was sullen as he lumbered into the therapy office. He was a big kid—not only tall, but obviously overweight. Clearly, this was not what he had in mind for a fun afternoon. He wore long pants and a long-sleeved shirt, so if any cutting behavior was occurring, Ben had hidden it. Most aspects of Ben seemed hidden, as he either grunted his answers or ignored the therapist entirely. Rapport building was going to be a challenge.

Surprisingly enough, Ben continued to attend therapy and seemed to relax a bit with each visit. He remained somewhat noncommunicative until a month before school was to begin. The therapist noted that Ben was getting more irritable and restless in sessions and she confronted him about this. Ben said, "Okay. I'm going to give this a chance," and gradually told the therapist an all-too-familiar story of bullying at school. A group of boys had targeted Ben because of his weight and sluggish movements. Taunting and name-calling in front of his peers was what Ben had to look forward to in September. These boys had already begun leaving messages on Ben's phone, letting him hear previews of coming attractions. Ben admitted that this was why he had started drinking and doing some minor cutting. He felt helpless to handle the situation and felt adults wouldn't understand or intervene.

THERAPIST: Ben, tell me what bothers you most about this bullying.

BEN: I hate feeling humiliated in front of the other kids. I know I'm ugly and overweight, but I don't need to be constantly reminded of it in public. I've tried so hard to lose weight this summer, but nothing seems to work.

THERAPIST: Ben, I'm curious. If this weren't a problem for you, what would you most like to focus your attention on?

BEN: I really wanted to play football and was actually good when I played Pop Warner in junior high. But it's too late.

THERAPIST: Maybe not. If you're willing to look at this goal, I happen to have a sports illustration that might help us get you there.

BEN: Sure. Why not?

The therapist drew the target and asked Ben what goals he wanted to reach in life in addition to playing football. He warmed up to the Pole Vault for Goals illustration and became more talkative than he had ever been in therapy. The therapist discovered that Ben wanted to go to college and become a physical education instructor. He felt he wanted to help other kids who experienced problems similar to his. He also had another goal: that he wanted a black sports car to drive to school.

THERAPIST: You have wonderful goals, Ben. Now let's see what steps will need to be taken for you to reach those goals. It's typically best to start with a low bar until you master vaulting over that with confidence.

BEN: Well, if I'm going to play football this year, I'd better call the coach when I get home to order my uniform.

THERAPIST: One of the first game rules we need to work on is establishing realistic plans for reaching your goals. The bar to play football this fall might be higher than you can vault over in a month. But let's set up a training plan.

Ben and his therapist thought through each of his goals, often resetting the timelines for raising the bars, as Ben tended to be impulsive. Ben talked with the football coach and found out what he would need to do to be on the team. He was invited to attend and participate in practices, but the coach clearly told him that he would not be able to play with the team this year. Ben had waited too late to begin training, but next year was a definite possibility. The coach shared with Ben that once he was in better shape, he definitely had the strength the coach wanted for the team. This encouraged Ben, and he had his mother take him to their primary care physician for the required physical. While Ben was there, the doctor helped him develop a plan for weight loss.

Diagnosis:	Adjustment disorder with depressed mood
Goals:	Learn to effectively deal with bullies
	Lose weight and build muscle
	Play sports
Interventions:	Social-skills training
	Self-defense training
	Consultation with physician and nutritionist for weight loss

Work with a physical trainer to guide his football
    training
Cognitive-behavioral therapy to help Ben cope
    with depressive feelings

Ben eagerly began to work on his goals, in spite of the bullies at school. As he ignored them and focused on "pole-vaulting" to reach these goals, they began to move on to other targets. As Ben experienced ever-growing success, particularly in sports, his grades began to improve and his affect became brighter. His mother was delighted to have her son back.

SUGGESTIONS FOR FOLLOW-UP

Ben continued in therapy for about six months, gradually increasing the time between visits. Since Ben had withdrawn due to the treatment by school bullies, he hadn't allowed others to help him. Once Ben saw that others were able and willing to coach him along, he began to accept their help in achieving his goals. Ben was given an assignment toward the end of his therapy to find community, school, and family resources that he could access when he needed help. One of the key components to anyone reaching their goals is to know when and who to ask for help and then be willing to examine their advice. Listening to a coach was something Ben had always resisted, but he now discovered it was exactly what was needed.

CONTRAINDICATIONS FOR USE

The concept of reaching goals is really applicable in any situation. Obviously, the bars need to be modified to be attainable. The therapist can guide this process. The Pole Vault for Goals illustration is really not contraindicated for any particular condition other than hatred of sports. Some clients have no interest in sports and would simply not find it to be something with which they could identify.

Chapter 14

The Spider Web

OBJECTIVE

The Spider Web illustration demonstrates how we can get caught up in the complexities of life. The client will be able to identify and sort through these complexities, which at times can feel like the sticky web strands that hold an insect as a prisoner. Eventually, the client will learn how to cut the web strands that hold them captive.

RATIONALE

Nothing is simple about the twenty-first century lives we lead. Sometimes the complexities are due to the pressures put on us by others, sometimes they are due to pressures we put on ourselves, and sometimes they are due to life itself—providing food, clothing, shelter, and so forth for ourselves and our families. These many pressures can mount up and overwhelm us to the point that we feel powerless to manage them. In fact, it can seem like they begin to manage us. At this point, we can begin to feel like the insect caught in a spider web.

The strands in a spider web are all intricately woven together in distinct patterns depending on the type of spider weaving them. The pressures and problems in our lives mimic that type of pattern. They tend to connect to one another in some way, and the pattern builds based on these connections. The pattern might change depending on the source of the problems. Unfortunately, we often get caught in the web almost before we realize what has happened. Some people may panic when they discover their situation and begin to fight against the web, trying to tear themselves out of it. This typically results in becoming more entwined than ever. In fact, in a real spider web, when

Published by The Haworth Press, Inc., 2006. All rights reserved.
doi:10.1300/5397_14

insects fight to get out, they get so wound up in the web, they eventually deplete their strength to fight and die, and become dinner for the spider.

When a spider begins to spin its web, it starts in the center and builds outward, one strand at a time. Initially, that web wouldn't be able to catch many insects. But as one row of the web grows into several, the spider is quite likely to entrap a fly. Humans always have pressures and stressors in their lives that demand attention. However, when we deal with them directly and in a timely manner, we often find them motivating and experience positive feelings about ourselves. When we try to circumvent these pressures and stressors, avoid them, or hope someone else will come along and rescue us, they tend to expand like the spider's web. The spider itself becomes this ominous demon that looms over us, waiting for the opportunity to devour us. It is the demon of the known or unknown consequences of what might befall us if we continue to be caught in its web.

How does this happen? Some of the ways in which people might find themselves getting trapped in a spider's web include lying to get out of uncomfortable situations, procrastinating when deadlines are due, trying to push their problems off on others, or simply avoiding taking any responsibility for things that need to be done. Each time a problem or stressor is avoided in some way, it tends to create a foundation for another web strand to be built upon, thereby increasing the likelihood of getting caught in the web. As people begin to realize they're getting stuck in a very unpleasant trap, they tend to panic. To deal with the panic, they either begin flailing about to try to fight their way out or they begin to feel hopeless and give up. Either way, they succumb to the trap and die.

In this case, dying may seem like a strong analogy, not pertaining to the real world. However, people can die in many ways. Loss of self-esteem and self-confidence, physical health, important relationships, self-respect, reputation, and hope for the future all are ways in which we can "die." Physical death can be a reality if people lose their health or turn to suicide.

The Spider Web illustration visually clarifies how the strands of pressure and stressors build upon one another. It helps clients see how one problem can lead to the next until they become overwhelmed with their situations. As the connections become clear, the client and therapist can work on helpful, creative solutions to begin cutting the web strands that hold the client prisoner. Relief is experienced as clients watch each strand being erased. When the strands are all cut away, the spider has no choice but to retreat. Dinner is no longer available.

THE SPIDER WEB
EXERCISE INSTRUCTIONS

Unless you have arachnophobia, you'll have no problems drawing The Spider Web illustration. Begin with the spider starting to spin its web (see Figure 14.1).

Although it may be difficult, as the client gives his or her history, begin to identify the web strands as the initial problems or stressors. This may be difficult, as the client may not have recognized how one poor choice, one unfortunate circumstance, or one negative behavior may have laid a foundation for additional strands of the web to be woven. If the client gets held up at this point, encourage him or her to continue; the therapist can help sort things out over time. Continue drawing strands of the web, labeling each strand as a problem or stressor which the client is experiencing (see Figure 14.2).

Examples of web strands might include the following:

- Lying
- Deceitful behavior
- Avoiding problem solving
- Unresolved anger
- Refusal to comply with medical treatment
- Procrastination when tasks are due
- Substance abuse

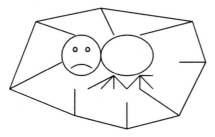

FIGURE 14.1. A spider spins its web.

Each of these problems is serious and may take some time to work through in therapy. Also, some clients may be resistant to examining the connections between these strands and their current experiences of emotional pain and discomfort. The final image of the Spider Web may make an impact that will help clients overcome any resistance to examining the interweavings of their history. Seeing oneself entrapped in the web can be a very powerful image (see Figure 14.3). The therapist will need to be prepared for strong reactions and focus on hope of relief as the strands are cut (see Figure 14.4).

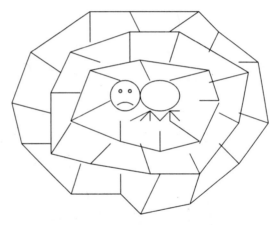

FIGURE 14.2. Each strand represents a problem or stressor.

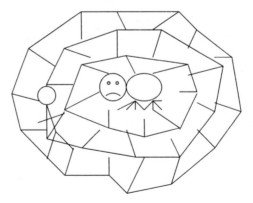

FIGURE 14.3. Show how individuals get caught in a web of stressors.

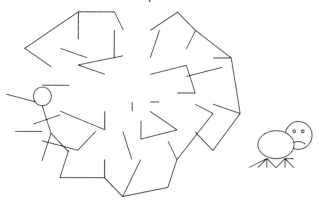

FIGURE 14.4. If the stressors are removed, the client can break free of the web.

What relief a client can experience when they visually see the web strands that have held them captive fall away, eventually sending the spider running!

VIGNETTE

Susan was a fifteen-year-old girl who began therapy at the recommendation of her high school guidance counselor. Susan had received three suspensions from school for fighting with other girls. The guidance counselor felt that Susan needed more intensive therapy than what she would be able to provide at school. Susan's mother brought her in and was obviously distressed over her daughter's situation. Even Susan was willing to admit that she would like for her life to be different and less problematic, but she didn't know how to change her situation.

Susan's parents were divorced when she was eight years old. Susan had little contact with her father, who had moved to another state. She had two younger sisters and her mother worked long hours to provide for the family. Susan's mother appeared to be a fairly passive individual who was permissive with her children rather than risking the conflicts she hated. As a result, all three girls had been in trouble at school when teachers had tried to set limits with them. As therapy began, Susan began revealing an all-too-common history.

Most of what she remembered about her family prior to the divorce regarded her parents arguing with each other. Sometimes her father would drink too much and the arguments with her mother occasionally turned physical. After her father moved away, Susan only saw him a couple of times a year. He rarely called and it wasn't uncommon to find only empty hopes for a birthday present. Susan denied being angry with her father. She stated she was more angry with her mother for driving him away. She was resentful at often having to assume child-care responsibilities for her younger sisters when she would rather be out with her friends. According to Susan, if her father were home, she would have more free time and could afford "cooler" clothes. Susan failed to perceive the inconsistencies of her remarks. The therapist said nothing at this point but noted the discrepancies for later.

THERAPIST: Susan, do you ever remember a time in your life when you were happy and things seemed to be going smoothly for you?

SUSAN: Before my parents split up. Even if they were fighting, I would just go outside and play with my friends. My mother ended all the good times with her constant nagging and whining.

THERAPIST: It sounds like you blame your mom for a lot of negative things that happened in your home.

SUSAN: If the shoe fits, wear it. And look at her now, she's still whining around all the time.

THERAPIST: How do you think that might relate to the problems you're having now?

SUSAN: Well, I learned from my mother that I have to stand up for myself; I can't count on *her.*

THERAPIST: Would it be fair to say that you're afraid of feeling defenseless?

SUSAN: Maybe.

THERAPIST: One of the things you told me earlier was that you like biology class and make good grades if you do your homework. I'm thinking of an illustration from biology that might help us look at what's going on in your life. You're not afraid of spiders, are you?

SUSAN: Of course not. I'm not afraid of anything.

THERAPIST: Susan, spiders are predators who spin webs to catch their prey. The webs start small and obviously get larger with each strand the spider spins. Eventually, the web is large enough to entrap insects, who will become the next meal unless freed from the web. It sounds to me that problems began when you were much younger and over the years have developed into a good-sized web that is keeping you stuck right now.

SUSAN: This is a gross example, but I understand what you're talking about. I told you earlier: I really don't like fighting and getting into trouble all the time, but I don't know how to stop. I don't want to be stuck in a web.

The therapist helped Susan begin to name the problem strands in the web, beginning at the center. She started with her mother's passive behavior, the divorce, and having to babysit her younger sisters. Blaming outward sources of her problems was as far as she could go on her own. The therapist began to gently ask if any of her own behaviors might be problematic for her. Initially, Susan responded with indignance, but once she was assured that she was not being blamed for her problems, she calmed down and agreed that her anger often got her into trouble.

She also confessed that sometimes she hated being at home so much that she lied to her mother, telling her she had to stay after school to finish homework when she actually went cruising with older friends. A couple of times she got caught, and her mother grounded her for a month. The third time this happened, Susan escaped out her bedroom window after dark to meet these friends at a local park. Because it was after the town curfew for young teens, Susan was picked up by a police officer and returned home with a stern warning to her mother to keep better track of her. As the web got larger, so did Susan's eyes as she began to see how far reaching her problems were becoming.

THERAPIST: Susan, let's talk now about the fighting at school with other girls. How did that begin and what's it about?

SUSAN: I wanted to try and fit in with this one group of girls. They're real popular at school and everyone wants to chill with them. I tried just being friendly, but they made fun of me because I don't have nice things. I took it for awhile and then got angry. In fact, I smacked one of these girls after school one day and gave her a black eye. The next day, the group came up to me and I thought I was toast. But they told me there was one way I could hang out with their group. If I would beat up this particular girl they didn't like and take the heat for it, that would prove that I was worthy to be part of their group. I thought, what the hell, and did it. I knew some great moves from watching my dad. The girl I beat up was scared out of her mind and I enjoyed the power plus I was now part of the in crowd. I just kept it up whenever anyone crossed me.

THERAPIST: It sounds like you have mixed feelings at this point. Although you enjoyed being with a more popular group of girls, you no longer like all the trouble you get into with the fighting.

SUSAN: I guess. And now they're starting to pressure me to do other things I don't want to do, like play sex games with their boyfriends and get alcohol for them.

Susan eventually developed enough trust in her therapist to reveal that one of the boyfriends had sexually molested her. She told her "friends" and was deeply wounded to find that they didn't care and only laughed about it. They were cruel enough to say they were glad it was her and not one of them. Susan was more than ready to leave this group of girls behind but had burned many bridges with other kids. She had started drinking to numb her feelings and was getting frightened that her life was so out of control. She was ready for help.

Diagnosis:	Adjustment disorder with mixed disturbance of conduct and emotions
	Parent-child relational problems
Goals:	Development of positive friendships
	More positive relationship with her mother and sisters
	Gain a better understanding of herself and how her own choices and behaviors contribute to her problems
	Stay out of trouble at school and with the law
Interventions:	Individual therapy to sort through feelings and behaviors
	Social skills training to better learn how to initiate positive peer relationships
	Family therapy to work on relationships with her mother and sisters
	Consultation with the school guidance counselor to devise a behavior plan for Susan at school

Coaching with Susan to help her learn behavior-
management strategies for herself

Encourage Susan's mother to engage in individual therapy herself and to enroll in a parenting
class

Over time, Susan admitted that she felt so unprotected by her parents that she had to put forth a tough persona to feel safe, including
being defiant with adults whom she didn't trust. Once she was able to
drop her guard, she began to see how her family situation, her own
negative choices and behaviors, and the stressful relationships she
had with peers all built upon one another to create a very large web indeed. And Susan did feel "stuck" in the web. As she and her therapist
applied the interventions they had agreed upon, Susan began to cut
the strands of her web. When they saw the spider turn and run because
he no longer had a web for his prey, they celebrated with a therapy
termination party!

SUGGESTIONS FOR FOLLOW-UP

Susan needed a good deal of help finding other kids who were willing to build healthy friendships with her. Her therapist made many
suggestions of community and school activities before Susan found
situations in which she felt comfortable. This also required many
phone calls and meetings with the school guidance counselor, who
was also eager to help. Susan's mom did find a therapist of her own
and began individual work in order to develop the strength she needed
to be a parent who could provide security for her children. Both therapists collaborated to help this family resolve past hurts and learn
healthier ways to cope with their situation.

Once she was old enough, Susan got a job, which helped her self-esteem immensely. After a great deal of therapy and planning, Susan set
up a meeting with her dad to ask him questions about the divorce and to
confront him about the neglect she had experienced from him. She
gave the meeting mixed reviews but felt good that she had developed
enough courage to initiate this contact. Susan also learned to use the
Spider Web illustration for self-evaluation. Whenever she began to feel
overwhelmed with problems, she would return to the illustration and

begin to ask herself to identify the strands that kept widening the web. She found that this helped her to be honest with herself and to address problems before she got swallowed up by the spider.

CONTRAINDICATIONS FOR USE

The Spider Web illustration is another one that could easily overwhelm clients with fragile ego strength. Seeing all of one's deficits and problems creating a web with the potential for serious discomfort is more than some people could handle. Also, the vision of being stuck in the web with a predator approaching and feeling unable to escape may trigger nightmares and flashbacks for clients who have experienced severe trauma in the past. Therefore, the Spider Web illustration should be avoided in these instances. Again, anyone with arachnophobia will likely be repulsed by this illustration and find themselves spending too much time and energy dealing with their fears to benefit from the concepts of the drawing.

Chapter 15

The Cracked Vase

OBJECTIVE

The Cracked Vase illustration simply demonstrates that beauty can be reconstructed from the broken pieces of our lives. That beauty may take a different shape and appearance from the original vase, but may be even more striking and valuable in the end.

RATIONALE

None of us get through life without some battle scars. As anyone in the helping professions knows, some people cope with these scars better than others. Genetic and environmental factors both contribute to our coping potential. In addition, education, training, and mentoring develop these natural traits to a level of optimal functioning. That is, for those individuals fortunate enough to have access to these resources. Abuse, neglect, and trauma intrude into the lives of way too many people, and damage is done. Particularly if these horrible events occur early in life, perspectives can get warped.

It is not uncommon for people to blame themselves for the bad events they've experienced. Maybe it feels that they have more control from that angle. Feeling out of control is unbearable for most individuals. Once people have internalized the ugliness they have experienced, it becomes extremely difficult to believe in beauty connected with themselves. What contributes to a sense of positive self-worth? Believing that we are unconditionally accepted and approved of leads to a sense of healthy pride in our creation. It is difficult to recapture this once it is lost. For some strange reason, one negative remark, look, or event can outweigh a hundred positive ones.

Published by The Haworth Press, Inc., 2006. All rights reserved.
doi:10.1300/5397_15

Abuse, neglect, and trauma are not the only factors involved in a sense of low self-worth. Some people, for various reasons, place an inordinate value on external appearances. They don't trust that their internal qualities are of value. Therefore, they place all their efforts into making their external qualities shine. It is impossible to maintain that forever. If nothing else, we all age with varying degrees of gracefulness and beauty. Apart from personal influences, U.S. culture focuses and prizes youth and beauty. Some people feel their lives are over with the discovery of the first wrinkle. Millions of dollars are spent each year on plastic surgery, beauty aids, and weight-loss programs, not to mention millions more on the latest fashions.

This desire to maintain a beautiful appearance often extends much farther than our bodies. It reaches out to the homes in which we live, including the furnishings and grounds. It touches our cars, our vacation spots, and our workplaces. The time and energy these objects require for maintenance is astronomical. The search for the perfect appearance can even lead to our choice of friends, as we make sure they are as or more beautiful than we are.

There is absolutely nothing wrong with the enjoyment of beauty. Beauty is one of the greatest enjoyments of our lives on this Earth. It can give us a sense of peace and hope. We can also achieve tremendous personal satisfaction when we participate in creating beauty for ourselves and others to enjoy. Beauty develops into a problem when we feel so internally barren that the appearance of beauty becomes the total focus of our lives. When we neglect the nurturance and growth of our spirits, our characters, our values, and our intellect for the sake of creating superficial beauty, we've lost something precious.

The Cracked Vase illustration addresses this issue of external beauty and encourages clients to consider beauty in a different way. We all start out in life as perfect vases. What baby isn't the most beautiful little being you've ever seen? It isn't long, though, before that baby grows up, learns to walk, and falls down—with scraped knees and tears resulting. Cracks begin to show up in our vases. Some of these cracks are very fine lines that we would need a magnifying glass to detect. Others are broad and bold. Some cracks are so severe that the vase breaks into pieces and the owner only hopes the superglue will keep it held together.

We can make several choices about cracked vases. We can ignore the cracks and just not care what they look like. We can admire the uniqueness of the cracks. We can carefully fill the cracks with new clay, refire them, paint them, and try to make them look new again. Alternatively, we can determine that the vase is so flawed, it's now worthless, and throw it in the trash. The Cracked Vase illustration helps clients to examine and acknowledge their "cracks." Then each of these choices can be evaluated. The end goal of the Cracked Vase illustration is to help clients come to value their "cracks" and believe that each "crack" can be transformed into beauty with such depth and richness they will wonder how they ever lived without it.

THE CRACKED VASE
EXERCISE INSTRUCTIONS

The nice thing about the Cracked Vase illustration is that even if it's not perfectly drawn, one can always just say it's a work of art. The whole purpose of the illustration is to help clients discover beauty in all circumstances. With that being said, first create a vase (see Figure 15.1). Discuss with the client what his or her idea of beauty and perfection looks like and what the meaning of beauty is to them personally. Then, relate the example of a beautiful little baby falling and scraping their knees, receiving the first crack in the vase. Next, draw another vase with cracks (see Figure 15.2).

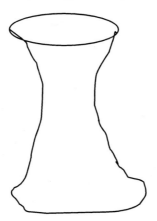

FIGURE 15.1. The uncracked vase.

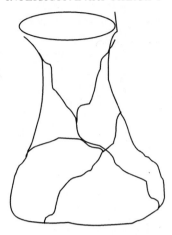

FIGURE 15.2. The beauty of the cracked vase.

Now have the client begin to label the cracks, the times when his or her beauty has been damaged in some way. The cracks may be due to his or her own choices or due to someone else knocking them off a shelf. Sometimes even the wind can blow over a vase, cracking it through no individual's fault. Process with the client what the cracks mean to him or her and how those cracks have affected the way the client lives life. If the client perceives the cracks in such a negative way that he or she can't function optimally, then help the client imagine the cracks from another perspective.

For example, Christopher Reeve was admired the world over for his handsome physique in the Superman movies. After being paralyzed in a riding accident, he developed new beauty in his tireless efforts to speak out on behalf of the handicapped. His encouragement and commitment to this cause drew many more people to admire him. He could easily have succumbed to self-pity about the fact that his handsome physique had been altered. Instead, he saw the cracks in his vase from a different perspective.

VIGNETTE

Lucy was a thirty-six-year-old housewife and mother of three children who came for therapy because of dissatisfaction with her life and a subsequent depression. Many things had occurred in her life to bring her to this point and Lucy could no longer carry the emotional load. As a young girl, Lucy had been stunningly beautiful. She had been very popular in school and had been voted homecoming queen in her senior year. She took good care of herself and had enjoyed the positive attention and admiring looks she received as a result.

The night after her senior prom, Lucy and some of her friends were involved in a car accident. The driver had been drinking and the front-seat passenger was killed. Lucy had been in the backseat and sustained a broken leg and a large gash across her face from a broken window. She eventually recovered physically, although the gash across her face left a very noticeable scar. Lucy never completely recovered emotionally from the death of her friend. The facial scar was a constant reminder of that event. Because Lucy felt a large part of her popularity had been based on her appearance, she became very self-conscious and began to withdraw more socially.

She went to college the next year and met Will, a "computer geek" who was thrilled that Lucy would even notice him. Lucy was depressed at that point and had developed the belief that no man whom she considered worthwhile would ever be attracted to her again. Although on some level, she knew this perspective was unfair to Will, she didn't care anymore. All that mattered was that she was no longer alone with her memories. Not caring led to an unplanned pregnancy in the second semester of her freshman year. Lucy dropped out of school to marry Will. Will genuinely loved Lucy and was determined to make the marriage work. He finished college and was soon hired by a tech company that offered him a very attractive salary.

Over the next few years, Will and Lucy had two more children and Lucy stayed home to care for them. With each pregnancy, she gained more weight and stopped taking care of herself in other ways as well. Although Lucy cared for Will and appreciated the good income he provided for the family, she had never developed a deep love or respect for him as her husband. She began to resent his success in life, as it highlighted her own feelings of inadequacy. The facial scar, the weight gain, and the stretch marks from childbirth all combined to make Lucy feel like the ugliest human being alive.

At thirty-six years of age, Lucy now had a sixteen-year-old daughter of her own who bore a striking resemblance to the stunning sixteen-year-old Lucy. As her daughter began attending school dances, having slumber parties with her girlfriends, and dating, Lucy's memories of the car accident were reignited. She began placing extraordinary limits on her daughter, who naturally resented them and fought back. Lucy and Will were also fighting more than ever, as she never communicated to him what was behind her behavior. Lucy was also remembering being the beautiful "belle of the ball" and her self-esteem plummeted. She hated going outside of the house and began to imagine that people all around her were making remarks about how ugly she looked. By the time she came for therapy, her depression was severe, she was ready to leave her husband, and her relationship with her children was becoming very strained and contentious.

THERAPIST: Lucy, you seem quite depressed. Let's review your symptoms and assess what we need to do about that.

LUCY: I can't remember when I wasn't depressed at this point, but it has definitely been getting worse the past six months. I feel like I should just finish what the car accident started.

After assessing the situation, the therapist determined that Lucy's symptoms of depression were indeed severe and that her suicidal thoughts needed to be taken seriously. The therapist recommended hospitalization for Lucy in order to ensure her safety and to begin her medical treatment. Lucy was desperate for help and was quite cooperative with this plan. Will was supportive and took her to the hospital, where she remained for a week. After her discharge, Lucy attended a partial hospitalization program for three weeks. She was feeling significantly better when she returned to her therapist to begin intensive work on all of the surrounding issues.

THERAPIST: I'm so glad to see you feeling better. Let's begin to explore the emotional and psychological factors that contributed to your depression.

LUCY: Definitely. I had no idea I had deteriorated to the level I had until I began the antidepressant medication and began to feel better. One of the things I realized in the partial hospitalization program was that I have never resolved my feelings of grief and loss from the car accident eighteen years ago. I had just buried those feelings and they came out in other ways.

THERAPIST: Now that you've started to reflect on that incident, what are some of those feelings that are resurfacing?

LUCY: I've been remembering how guilty I felt that I never spoke up to ask that someone sober drive us home. I was very worried about my popularity in those days and never wanted anyone upset with me. I'm also realizing that I felt the only reason people really liked me was because I was pretty. After the accident, I felt no one would ever want to be around me again.

THERAPIST: Those are very powerful insights. Where do you think you got the idea that the only reason people liked you was because of your appearance?

LUCY: Well, I remember people always staring at me and then remarking how pretty I was, even my family. I never recall anyone commenting on what a nice personality I had or that I was doing well in school. It seemed like a natural conclusion to make that being pretty was the most important thing. And now I see my daughter experiencing the same thing. I'm also feeling guilty that I've never tried to affirm her in other areas of her life. I've been reliving my own childhood through her, once again enjoying the attention of being pretty. I can't stand to look at myself in the mirror anymore.

THERAPIST: I understand that you are quite an accomplished pianist and that you have a very creative side expressed in the decoration of your home. Would you be able or willing to accept any compliments from others in those areas?

LUCY: No, I don't believe I could. I would likely just think they were feeling sorry for me because of my ugliness and trying to divert attention to something else to make me feel better.

THERAPIST: Let's see if we can begin to develop a different perspective on your situation through an illustration.

The therapist drew a picture of a flawless vase and worked further with Lucy to explore what it felt like to her and meant to her to have been such a beautiful young woman. Lucy began to cry as she recognized that she had never developed many interests or depth of character beyond that beauty. Because of all the attention she had received, the beauty seemed enough. Then the therapist redrew the vase and began to draw the cracks, having Lucy label them as they appeared.

LUCY: The cracks in the vase directly relate to the scar on my face and the stretch marks on my body. That's obvious. But I'm also seeing that my marriage to Will has felt like a crack. I feel guilty even saying that because he has been a faithful and caring provider all these years. I have to admit I haven't given much back. Also, dropping out of college was another crack. You're right. Will must have told you about the music and interior decorating. If I hadn't dropped out, I would have pursued those interests in college. The most recent cracks have been the fighting with my daughter and the depression. The suicidal thoughts scared me and they were definitely a fracture in the vase. It almost fell completely apart and I could never have fixed it again.

THERAPIST: The cracks in your vase have definitely been very painful and have had a major impact on your life. But I wonder if we could try looking at them from a different perspective. Can beauty come from the cracks themselves?

LUCY: You're a miracle worker if you can pull that off.

THERAPIST: Not at all. Let's just turn the vase around instead of looking at it head-on. Notice how interesting those cracks are, the unique quality they bring to the vase. It's now not like any other vase on the market in any way. Let's talk about how those cracks have brought depth, wisdom, and interest into your life.

As they processed the cracks in this manner, Lucy began to brighten up, realizing that the vase now had more than just a pretty surface. Lucy realized that she had gained much wisdom and knowledge through these cracks, but that she had only attributed negative qualities to them. After taking the time to thoroughly look at the vase from this new perspective, the therapist asked Lucy if she would like to make any changes to the vase, truly making it her own.

Diagnosis:	Major depression, severe
	Parent-child relational problems
	Partner relational problems
Goals:	Improve her self-esteem
	Resolution of depressive symptoms
	Improved relationships with her family
Interventions:	Initially, hospitalization and subsequent treatment of severe depression
	Medication management and collaboration with her psychiatrist

Individual therapy to process issues of grief and loss
Marital therapy to improve her relationship with
　Will
Family therapy to improve her relationships with
　her children, especially her daughter
Individual therapy to help Lucy with self-actual-
　ization

Lucy decided after a time that although she appreciated what she had learned from the cracks, she did want to make some changes. She wanted to fill in and repaint some of the cracks. For Lucy, this meant returning to college and finishing her degree in interior decorating. She also resumed her piano lessons. Lucy made the major decision to contact a plastic surgeon to see if any cosmetic repairs could be made to her facial scar. She joined a weight-loss program and began exercising.

SUGGESTIONS FOR FOLLOW-UP

Lucy was feeling that she needed to make up for lost time, so to speak. Her therapist continued working with her to help her pace the changes she wanted to make. Lucy needed to face her feelings about how she would handle improving her appearance. That had been such a loaded issue for her in the past. They needed to help prepare Lucy for the attention she would once again receive on that level.

Lucy also decided to make the commitment to work on her marriage with Will. She wanted to make it a satisfying first-rate relationship instead of just settling for second best. Will was delighted and agreed to do his part in this process. All of these changes took time, and Lucy needed her therapist's support in finding resources as she pursued her goals. Lucy's changes also led to adjustments that needed to be made with her children. Her oldest daughter, in particular, benefited from individual therapy of her own.

CONTRAINDICATIONS FOR USE

Like most of the other illustrations in this book, the Cracked Vase illustration is not appropriate for someone with a fragile internal structure. The focus on keeping external appearances beautiful may be a defense mechanism to hide an inadequate and broken interior. It would be cruel and unethical to tear away the superficial layers of beauty and expose the damaged goods beneath. Prior to using the Cracked Vase illustration, the therapist will need to help the client develop a solid foundation of positive coping strategies and a sense of self-worth that can stand up to the challenge of such deep personal exploration.

Epilogue

The end of this book is really the beginning. Hopefully, it has sparked the reader's imagination and demonstrated how clients can gain helpful insight into their situations with simple yet purposeful drawings. The drawings are only limited by the creativity of the therapist and the client. These drawings provide a point of coming together for all involved, a foundation on which to build both the relationship and the healing experience.

Published by The Haworth Press, Inc., 2006. All rights reserved.
doi:10.1300/5397_16

References

Basic Behavioral Science Task Force of the National Advisory Mental Health Council (1996). Basic behavioral science research for mental health: Perception, attention, learning, and memory. *American Psychologist,* 51(2), 133-142.

Kalyuga, S., Chandler, P., and Sweller, J. (2000). Incorporating learner experience into the design of multimedia instruction. *Journal of Educational Psychology,* 92(1), 126-136.

Kaplan, H.I. and Sadock, B.J. (eds.) (1989). *Comprehensive Textbook of Psychiatry/ V.* Baltimore, Hong Kong, London, Sydney: Williams and Wilkins.

Mayer, R.E. and Sims, V.K. (1994). For whom is a picture worth a thousand words? Extensions of a dual-coding theory of multimedia learning. *Journal of Educational Psychology,* 86(3), 389-401.

Moreno, R. and Mayer, R.E. (2002). Verbal redundancy in multimedia learning when reading helps listening. *Journal of Educational Psychology,* 94(1), 156-163.

Mousavi, S.Y., Low, R., and Sweller, J. (1995). Reducing cognitive load by mixing auditory and visual presentation modes. *Journal of Educational Psychology,* 87, 319-334.

Tindall-Ford, S., Chandler, P., and Sweller, J. (1997). When two sensory modes are better than one. *Journal of Experimental Psychology: Applied,* 3(4), 257-287.

Published by The Haworth Press, Inc., 2006. All rights reserved.
doi:10.1300/5397_17

Index

Page numbers followed by the letter "f" indicate figures.

Published by The Haworth Press, Inc., 2006. All rights reserved.
doi:10.1300/5397_18